Seasonal Magic
Diary of a Village Witch

Paddy Slade

Seasonal Magic
Diary of a Village Witch

©1997 Paddy Slade

ISBN 1 86163 0190

Cover design by Paul Mason
Cover photograph Bob Slade
Internal illustrations by Paddy Slade

Published by:

Capall Bann Publishing
Auton Farm
Milverton
Somerset
TA4 1NE

Contents

Foreword

With general interest in the occult burgeoning in the last twenty years, it is small wonder that the book shops are overrun with information on every conceivable aspect of the subject. However, for every twenty books published only one will have the undeniable stamp of authority, which is why I am writing a foreword for this book and not the other nineteen.

About thirty books a month land on my desk for review and it is often a struggle to find something to say about them. Most are written by people who, unlike Paddy, appear to have little in the way of serious magical training other than reading other people's books. It makes a great change when you find one that is written with humour, genuine knowledge and a deep love of the subject itself, and as a bonus, a bona fide 'village witch'. There are not many of them left.

Witchcraft has an incredibly ancient pedigree that reaches back into the early palaeolithic times. There are those who regard it merely as a remnant of the mystery religions that flourished in the golden age of the Mediterranean cultures, and it may well be that some aspects of these faiths gradually found their way into the practice of the Craft. Certainly much of the Greek herbal and healing law used in the temples of Aesculapius at Epidaurus can be discerned in the potions and practices of the witches. But in the main I think it must be acknowledged that the real basis of their religion stems from the shamanic beliefs which are depicted with such strength and beauty in the cave paintings of Lascaux, Les Eyzies and at Santander in Northern Spain.

As Paddy says in her book, most people think of witches as being part of a coven or group of thirteen, but this is a fairly late idea that began about the early sixteen hundreds. For the most part witches worked alone because it was safer and because of the danger of travelling long distances - the next village could well be a day's or even two day's walk away. The larger the group, the

1

more danger of betrayal. Certainly there were groups, indeed some whole villages were of the craft, including the squire and the priest, but they were the exception rather than the rule.

Within the pages of this book you will find genuine practices, rituals, spells, chants and information that have come down, mouth to ear in the traditional way. There are different kinds of witch; the Traditional, and such a one is the author of this book; and there are the Family witches where the practice is kept within blood members of one or at the most two families within a certain radius. The author belonged to one such family but is now prepared to share her knowledge, mainly to counteract some of the misinformation so freely disseminated. These are the oldest and purest forms, but there are also the more modern practitioners such as the Alexandrian and Gardnerian.

From earliest times up to the late thirteenth century witchcraft was still practised at one level or another in almost every village in England. After that time it went underground but it left behind a plethora of old folkways that even now persist, and keep our heritage alive. The "Obby Oss" of Padstow, the Verderer's Dance with the participants dressed in forest green and bearing antlers; the Old Tup ceremonies where a Ram is dressed up and made 'king' of the festivities. The Maypole and the Floral Dance, the more sinister Sword Dances and their "teasers" and many, many more.

In reading this book, you will be awakening race memories of Merrie England, one that has almost passed away, for it is nothing more than the Diary of a Country Witch. It will take you through an entire year of deceptively simple Craft workings, teach you the working spells that your ancestors knew and probably used themselves.

A village witch did not simply work magic, she healed, she advised, she dowsed for water and for lost articles, she was a midwife and a vet, a layer out of the dead and a gatherer of herbs. She worked the weather, raised winds for the sailors and calmed them down again. She found wives for the men and husbands for the girls and above all she worshipped the great primeval Mother

Goddess and arranged her life around those titanic tides of life and death over which SHE has always ruled.

For me, reading Paddy's book has been a comfort because it means that the old ways have not entirely vanished, that there are a few, a very few, village witches left out there. This is a distillation of old wisdom from the heart, without pretence, without a need to "get across a message", an offering of knowledge from the long ago, to the here and now. Because of my own connections I can vouch for the validity of what is written here. Practices differed from village to village but there was an underlying thread that bound the Craft together, not just throughout England but throughout Europe as well. A witch in Brittany worked in pretty much the same way as did the witch in Cornwall or Devon. Civilisation has swept us along in its wake, but in the villages of England some things never change.

Dolores Ashcroft Nowicki

The Widow's Story

OR

How This Book Came to be Written

Once upon a time, there was a widow who lived in a tiny village, perched high above a fast flowing, very deep river.

She lived alone, for both of her sons were married, and very busy increasing the world population but she often had friends who dropped in for a chat and stayed for a week or six. She was, you understand a very tolerant and good natured widow.

Also living in the cottage was a rather large, well-tempered ginger cat named Redbelkin, as opposed to Grimalkin, and everyone knows that cats of that name are anything but good tempered. Red had two great delights, food and having his tummy rubbed. Also, and at the same time, he tolerated a rather upper class German Shepherd bitch, of quite ferocious behaviour, who disliked men of whatever kind and those who rode motorbikes and wore black leather in particular. This was unfortunate, because the widow liked riding motorbikes herself so the lady had to accustom herself to lumping it.

The widow had not always lived in this rather cosy cottage. When her sons were young, she had, of necessity, to move around a lot, circumstances preventing her from staying in one place too long. Consequently, she had both seen and lived in, much of the beautiful country in which she lived. As they grew older, her sons surprised friends by the number of times they said as they themselves drove round the country, "Oh. We used to live round here."

She was, naturally, a worthy widow - much of her life was spent caring for other people's grannies (who did not always appreciate her kind of assistance, hence the temporary nature of most of her residences.)

Sometimes she looked after their dogs or horses, at which she was considerably better, and even, if she was very lucky, they allowed her to catalogue their libraries.

During these peripatetic years, she began to learn about herbs and plants and trees, and water and stones. She spent much of her time when she was not actually working visiting Hill forts, or Earthworks or stone circles, dancing with the wind which sang about the stones. She talked to trees and flowers, horses and cows, cats and dogs, and generally anything which would listen. Perhaps some people though her a trifle eccentric but as she never caused anyone any harm, they generally left her to her own devices.

She was, in case you haven't already guessed, A WITCH!

She had, at that time, a smart, rather racy, little yellow broomstick which she affectionately called "Herm". She rather liked cross country roads. She was often seen racing about her beloved countryside astride her broomstick.

Well anyway, to return to the matter in hand, she eventually settled in the cottage which I have already mentioned and got down to the serious business of being a (reasonably good) witch.

People came to her with their headaches, their corns and their unsatisfactory love affairs and asked her to solve these problems for them. So, being the tender hearted person she was, she would go into her garden, a riotous gathering of herbs, flowers and vegetables, all mixed up together and harvest what she needed. In many cases, this had to be done at certain times of the month - so the cures were by no means instant. Then she would concoct potions and cures and weave spells, (which were ALWAYS nice ones) ((unless someone made her very cross). Not all of her spells worked, but then they rarely do, but at least she tried.

The widow spent most of her days pottering about the house and garden or visiting ancient sites. Occasionally, she would host an extremely civilised dinner party for her friends, and even more occasionally, an extremely riotous bottle party for anyone who cared to turn up, so long as they came armed with an appropriate bottle of falling-down water.

Well, One day, the calm and peace of her simple existence was shattered by the arrival of an important television personage, who announced that he wished to make a programme, including a large part about herself. She was rather surprised at this, but after due consideration, like how much he was prepared to fork out, she agreed to take a part. It couldn't do any harm. Could it?

The arrangements proceeded, as arrangements are apt to do, and suddenly the widow's house was overrun by large cameramen, sound-recordists and other bodies of all descriptions, who usually are involved in such an undertaking. Some seemed to be along for the ride, but most appeared to know what they were doing which was much more than the widow did.

Not only did she find herself in the middle of a film, but also she seemed to spend a lot of time making tea and cucumber sandwiches, (it was in the middle of summer) and home-made scones and strawberry jam and clotted cream from the local farm and other such delights - all of which she found just a little trying.

The film was duly made and shown on National Television and the widow settled down to her quiet life once more. But no!!! Hundreds of letters poured through her letterbox; the telephone rang monotonously, and people arrived on her doorstep from all over the country. They all seemed to have insolvable problems. The widow tried to accept this with what looked like stoical complacency but under her breath she could be heard muttering acid comments about Walt Disney and his bloody magic wands.

Then people began to say "*Why don't you write a book?*" and eventually this cry became so frequent (and tiresome) that one day she sat down and started to write. The following is the result Now, the widow's philosophy was "*be careful what you ask for, because you might get it.*" Well, you asked for it and now you're going to get it.

Karen Slade

6

Introduction

This book is about seasonal magic, that is, the stuff used by country witches. It is not black nor white, this magic, although perhaps it can get a little grey at times. More often, because it is of the Earth, it is green or brown, the colours of nature.

I do not believe in Black Magic. I do not believe in White magic. I only believe in MAGIC, which so far as I am concerned is a type of electro-magnetic current, rather like electricity, which can be used for either good or bad, depending upon the intent of the user. The only Black Magic I really know of is a rather good box of chocolates of which I am very fond.

I'm not even sure what Black Magic is but I have a niggling feeling that it owes much to D. Wheatley and A. Crowley, neither of whom knew much about witches. Of course, both black magic and the two aforementioned gentlemen owe a great deal to two other gentlemen of a far earlier time, the authors of *Malleus Malificarum*, Kramer and Sprengler of whom it has been said, that *"if magicians did not know how to worship the devil before reading it, they certainly did after doing so"*. Wheatley and Crowley appear to have culled most of their knowledge from the transcripts of the witch trials and these were the result of what happens when sexually frustrated men allow their imaginations to run riot, forcing poor, illiterate old women, who were for the most part not witches, to confess to anything to relieve the agony inflicted upon their bodies and minds.

That "black" magic delights the press, there is no doubt. They blithely ignore explanations given in television programmes and magazine interviews and print anything sensational they can find, which usually has little to do with witchcraft and a great deal to do with so-called 'satanism' or more often, just plain, unpleasant paedophilia of which more churchmen, scout masters and choir masters are guilty than are witches.

I shall probably be in some very hot water for saying this, but one only has to read the papers. Tit for Tat.

We witches are followers of the Old Religion, practised on Earth since man began to think and very certainly before any established religion found it necessary to fill the world with evil and devils, Devil derives from the Sanskrit word for Deva, which meant "Shining One". It is odd that one of the early meanings of the word 'black' was also "shining".

After the showing of the television programme "*Earth Magic*" with which I had the honour to be associated, one critic who obviously thought he was extremely clever asked, "Why, if they are so innocent, do they make a pact with the Devil?"

The short answer is that we don't. Not in blood, urine or any other unmentionable substance. The Devil, dear Sir, is anti-Christ. Witches do not believe in Christ, except as one of the very great teachers. Since man was a gatherer of berries, a scavenger of meat and a follower of herds, he has worshipped the Earth, who gave and gives him all his sustenance; Water, without which he could not live and because it reflects the Earth. He worshipped the Moon, which gave him light in darkness. An Irish friend once said that he worshipped the Moon before the Sun because the Moon was there when it was dark. Much later, he, the Man Kind, learned to worship Fire and then the Sun and this is when sacrifice began. The Great Goddess, who GIVES life, does not require life to be taken in Her worship.

Many witches nowadays claim to worship something beyond our forefather's knowledge. Or is it? They say that they look to the Light Beyond the Light. But then, why did our old ones break their backs building Silbury Hill, the great Long Barrows and the vast Henges? They must have had a reason far beyond anything we know, or perhaps one we are only just beginning to understand.

Going back to the usual idea of witchcraft, it is claimed that in our "covens" we worship our MALE leader, in the guise of a goat. The rather nasty Goat of Mendes, who was supposed to be the

8

Devil. Yes, we give honour to a Horned One, but in this part of the world He usually has antlers. Horns were an ancient symbol of authority, even Moses was traditionally supposed to have them. Horned Ones convey FERTILITY, whether they be goats, rams, stags or bulls. Most ancient religions worshipped a male creature equipped with horns, they were supposed to represent the continuing survival of the tribe. The Goat God, Pan, is the Helper and Comfort of the creatures of the Greenwood as is our own Herne.

Covens are and were led by women, not men, and the village witch worked by herself. She had no need of a coven, which is merely part of the Latin word meaning "to gather", it also implied a 'fraudulent' gathering. It is difficult enough to gather thirteen people nowadays, at a specific time and date, especially if that date falls in the middle of the week. At a time of curfew, when one needed to cover miles across other people's land - and could be prosecuted, beaten and deported for doing so - it would have been practically impossible, unless as has been said, the group was a family or village one.

There are witch groups today who meet on "the nearest Saturday." To a traditional, hereditary witch, this is nonsense. One either works to the proper times and tides or not at all, with as many, or as few, dedicated people as can come. You worked clothed, not that silly phrase "Sky Clad", because no tribe, primitive or otherwise, goes to meet its God unclothed.

Even if they cover themselves with leaves, mud or paint, feathers or strips of leather, they array themselves with something. Gardner began this in the fifties, because he was himself a nudist and thought it would be fun to include nudity in his rituals. The phrase "Naked shalt thou be in thy rites" is an idea put about by the church, it was never part of witch lore. Witches were usually poor, had one garment into which they were stitched and which was worn until it fell off. They would not risk losing it by hanging it on a bush and having to run when their rite was interrupted by the militia.

We do not finish the evening with any type of sexual act, whether it is called the Great Rite or not, and we do not fornicate with a Goat. The Goat is to do with Mediterranean cults, being one of the few animals able to survive on barren summer hills.

Let me say something here about the Great Rite. It was the sacred marriage of the God to the Earth, through the medium of the Goddess. A boy and girl, young but both at exactly the same stage of knowledge and development performed this rite, in deep reverence. The ritual known as "Drawing Down the Moon" had made sure that the young woman was at her most fertile time, so that a child would be conceived. More about that later. It might well have been that, during the feast following the rite, in the days when this was done to ensure the fertility of the Earth, there was a general free for all, but that also was part of the celebration of fertility.

This rite should never be part of an initiation ceremony, because it causes an imbalance. Whichever is the more experienced performer, whether it be the priest or priestess, takes on a dangerous amount of Karma for the one to be initiated.

Gardens

I have a book on my bookshelf, and there are many more, which will tell you that a witch's garden is an overgrown, joyless and probably sunless place. I have seen many such, usually in the suburbs, full of old bicycles, hamburger cartons and various excreta. The walls, if there are walls, are covered with ivy, dark, dusty and dismal. I had no idea so many witches lived in suburbia. The only plants that grow are henbane, Deadly and Enchanter's Nightshade and Bryony. Not to mention , of course, Mandrake. I"d like to be able to grow this stuff, but I"ve only seen it once, half way up a mountain in Wales.

Perhaps you should see my garden. At the moment the front is a little overgrown, a vast juniper sprawls over most of it, but I haven"t the heart to cut it back. Everything shoots up with such exuberance that perhaps it does look untidy, the jasmine, roses and lemon balm do run riot. It faces South-West, is at the top of a steep hill and is sunny for most of the day.

The back garden has a lawn which came out, quite unexpectedly in the shape of the Goddess, with a clear spring running through it. I planted some sports of the Pink Almond along one fence, which have grown into trees. These flaunting, exuberant pink masses of froth were grafted onto cherry stumps. The 'sports' have reverted to type but I"ve never yet managed to get the cherries, the birds get 'em first. If I try to grow hedges, the sheep and horses eat the saplings. There is asparagus and a few vegetables growing among the other plants. Bulbs in spring, flowers and herbs all through the summer and not a deadly nightshade in sight.

All the plants known to keep witches away thrive in my garden. I have a ten foot Angelica and my poor little Monkshood gets smothered each year by Soapwort and Melilot. Totally open and sunny, and joyless? You should see my grandchildren, sons, their wives and others playing cricket there. Or splashing in the pool. We have supper out there, on warm summer evenings, watching the balloons flying up the valley and we do rites, not secretly, but with half the village watching, along with the cows, sheep, horses, buzzards, foxes, badgers, swifts, wrens and robins.

After the programme "*Earth Magic*" many people came to ask me questions and find out about the Craft. One man rode over quite a lot of England calling at every village with a name like mine. There are at least three of them, well spread apart, such enterprise demanded at least a cup of tea. He joined us for lunch, along with a lovely girl who had driven down from Scotland on the same quest. One of the ideas I keep having to correct is the idea that the Anglo-Saxon word "wicca" means "Craft of the Wise." Wicca is the Anglo-Saxon word for witch, see Sweet's *Anglo Saxon Dictionary*. It was a word of abuse, for they did not like the supernatural, although they were very superstitious. It means, "bent and twisted."

Eventually I began a teaching group and some of these people came to rites. Before this could happen, we had to have a series of lessons in ritual etiquette. They had to learn their left from their right for a start; how to hold and pass a cup and how to behave in a circle.

We taught them a simple dance, passing right and left shoulders. Oh, what a muddle. Perhaps because we did a lot of country dancing at school, (by this I do not mean American square dancing but ancient dances like *Sir Roger de Coverley*, and *Strip the Willow*), I have never found difficulty in weaving dances. But children are no longer taught these very useful little bits of information and grown ups, unless they have been in the Services, do not know how to move in a body.

This dance is quite important and we use it a lot, so I persevere, perhaps one day we"ll actually weave a proper lattice work around the Maypole, one can only hope. Now it is one thing getting people to stand in a circle, alternate sexes if possible, but getting men to face to the left and women to the right often means going round and forcibly shoving them in the right direction. Then, horror of horrors, they need to move the way they are facing, AND, PASS FIRST LEFT SHOULDER THEN RIGHT. Some insist on turning in small circles or simply stopping and allowing everyone else to flow round them, causing more confusion and a bunch of very unhappy would-be magicians can be left twirling madly in a corner. And they have to do this to music, keeping time with the beat and touching hands, and looking into eyes. Oh, boy.

We practised passing the cup, which must be done with both hands - one at the base and the other at the rim. So they put their hands over yours and wonder why you don't let go. We usually do not have a priestess taking the cup round but it might come to that. The trouble is, hereditary witchcraft does not have priestesses.

The passing of the plate can really cause bother if everyone is not reminded what to do each time. There is only one way to do this so that each person keeps both hands at the rim. That is, to pass the plate to the person on your left, no not the right dear, left. Rings and watches, except that watches should not be worn in a rite. Having taken it in both hands, the chap then offers it back to you. No you do not take it back, poppet, you merely take your piece of oatcake. He then passes it to the lady on his left, and she offers it back to him, and so on. All is well. One would think.

Except that some try to take their piece, put it in their mouth and pass the plate on. Some take it with one hand, take their small piece and pass it and some try to hold their oatcake in two fingers while passing the plate. I have watched, dumbstruck, (or nearly) while the plate whizzes around the circle with no-one getting a share but some goes onto the floor. There is nothing to do then but firmly take it oneself, gritting one's teeth, and keeping a firm grip and scowling horribly at anyone who tries to take it away, offer it round the hard way.

One needs to school one's group so that, when the circle is being opened, they actually move out of the way. I made sure of this, early in the group's being by snapping,"One pace forward, march." In a small room the circle must be as big as possible but they must learn not to stand like rocks so that you cannot get past. If one has to elbow them, violently, in the ribs it does not help in the construction of a circle of peace and harmony, a place guarding against unbalanced force, if the priestess is muttering imprecations under her breath.

We go for walks in the summer, round the fields nearby, so that people can learn about trees and herbs. It is necessary to know which tree is which, not only by the shape of their leaves but their general overall shape, so that one can recognise them at a distance and in winter. Some of the work we do requires this knowledge.

The study of witchcraft requires a knowledge of herbs, what they look like and how they are used. One needs to know what the clouds look like and what they foretell. The difference between barley and wheat, cow parsley and sweet cecily. The first of these will make you sick the second is a wonderful addition to gooseberries and rhubarb, cutting down the acidity and letting you use less sugar, you still need some, unless you happen to be a masochist.

I have always maintained that if one is set upon studying astrology one should have at least a nodding acquaintance with the major constellations, which means night study. Not one of the zodiacal signs or constellations are in the sky at the appropriate time, they are nearly all below the Northern or Eastern horizon. The Zodiac was conceived by a Zoroastrian priesthood who lived in Persia, a large country which spans some ten degrees of Latitude, namely 25^0 - 35^0 North. I have lived in Iraq and know that the relevant signs ARE in the sky at the right time. Britain is a very small series of islands which are located between 50 and 55 degrees (sixty if you count Shetland) and we do not have the same night sky.

A study of the main stars which make up these constellations is not only useful but very fulfiling. It gives one a sense of proportion to know just how far away and how enormous they are. I am sure that Stonehenge was built for the study of stars and never had anything to do with the rising of the Sun at the Summer solstice so beloved of modernish druids.

We do not worship the Moon now, we know that the Moon is a reflection of the Earth. What we see in the Moon is the aspects of our Lady Mother the Earth. We relate the first quarter to the Spring, Dawn and the Maiden. The Full to Summer, Midday and the Mother. The last quarter to Autumn, Evening and the Crone, and DO NOT FORGET, the Dark to Winter, Midnight and the Dark Goddess. the Goddess of Death and Re-birth, the Goddess Facing Both Ways. I get somewhat aggravated by the insistence of modern witches that there are only Three aspects of the Goddess. There are FOUR seasons, FOUR major times of day and at least FOUR major times of life. Birth, puberty, the menopause and death.

Why, then, is this very important stage of the Moon and the Earth and the Goddess ignored. I think it is because we have been programmed to ignore it. It makes us think of things we would rather not know about. Death is a mystery, deliberately made into a terror by those who should have known better. Ancient people, including the Celts, did not fear Death, they knew that it was the one certainty in life, the only way it could be frightening was to meet it with fear. If it is met with courage, and the Celts worshipped courage above all else, there should be nothing to fear. It is what comes just before, the manner of Death and what comes after, the real mystery which can be frightening. So, people, accept the Dark aspect of the Goddess. She is important.

It is a strange thing when, so far as we know, Earth is the only planet yet known which can support life, it is considered to be heretical to offer our worship to Her. One would imagine that all people who on Earth do dwell, would sing, not unto the Lord in cheerful voice, but to the Goddess who actually allows them to live. This is what we do.

We worship our Goddess, the Earth Mother, not by destroying her children, be they animal or vegetable or even mineral, but doing what we can to protect and cherish. We do not make blood sacrifices, we do not corrupt innocents and we make no effort to proselytize. If people want to join us, well and good and if they meet our somewhat exacting standards, we will teach them all we can, but we do not go out into the highways and byways to harry those whose beliefs are not ours.

There are those who under the guise of witchcraft, do these things. There are those who delight in crippling cats and children. Those who take and cause others to take drugs. Those who trail a faint smell of sulphur about their persons. They may be degenerate, obscene, delinquent and downright and demonstrably evil, but they are not witches.

The following chapters give some idea of what witchcraft really means.

Chapter One

SAMHAINE
October 31st

When the leaves begin to fall, we get
ready for the start of the Pagan year. We
play the game of "Catch the Leaf." which is
not so easy as you might think. Just as you
clutch one, the heat from your hands causes a
little thermal causing the leaf to rise and swirl
away. I usually find myself flat on my front in
some muddy place trying hard not to cuss
because that would be bad magical practice.

As the trees begin to show their skeletons and the first
frosts, the "hoar" frosts, whiten the grass, the only really
green tree left is the Holly, and of course, the ivy climbing
round the bare trunks. There are yews, cedars and some pines,
but we do not count those. For this is the time of Samhaine, when
the Holly Lord comes back from the Greenwood to protect us
throughout the winter.

This is the end of the year and also the beginning. Because we are
working with the continuing tides of Nature, we must finish one
thing before beginning another. So, we begin with an ending.
Samhaine is a Nature festival, one of the four very ancient rites
and with Beltaine in May, by far the most important.

Our ancient ancestors had only two seasons, Winter, which began
with the frosts, and Summer, which began with the Hawthorn
blossom. There is another version of this. Summer begins with the
Elder blossom and winter with the berries. The other two rites are
Imbolc or Oimelc, when the lambs are born, the ewes come into

milk and the snowdrops show themselves and Lughnasad, which is about the beginning of the harvest.

The other rites are solar ones and were imposed on the Old Religion; not in any arbitrary way but in the nature of tribal development, and evolution of a theme. The times of these eight rites are almost equally divided. Seven weeks from a solar to a nature rite and six from nature to solar, giving us four equal divisions of thirteen weeks in a year.

There are two explanations for the word Samhaine. The first and most accepted, is that it is Old Irish pronounced Sawen or Saven, and dates from the time when the surplus stock had to be killed, both to provide meat for the winter months and to preserve the limited supply of keep for the stock animals.

It is the time when the veil between the Otherworld and this one is said to be thinnest, this is connected with the spilling of so much blood. It is, therefore, considered to be the best time to contact those ancestors who have gone before. Not the newly dead, you must understand. They are too busy, or they should be, finding out about their new lives. It is cruel to keep calling them back to find out where they left the silver, or where Auntie May put the brooch you know she left to her favourite niece. The ones we call are the Old Ones, the tribal elders, who have had time and space to adjust and assimilate the knowledge which only they can pass on.

The second explanation and the one I think most likely is that the Greeks wrote about and thought very highly of, a priesthood whom they called "Samethoi", a pre-Celtic Shamanic brotherhood who, at the time of the first frosts, entered the Otherworld, probably through the round hills, to conduct the souls of the newly dead and to bring back knowledge. They were rather like the Egyptian and Chaldean Priests of the Dead. They were not Druids, who were possibly Zoroastrian, and came from Persia and joined up with the Celts on their long trek westward.

They were the priesthood of the former inhabitants of these islands, those who built Silbury Hill, the Long Barrows and some

17

of the henges. Nor were they famous for blood-letting, which incidentally, was usually solar not Earth Goddess orientated. Strangely enough though, the date of this descent and the slaughter of the animals was November the 11th, by the old calender, a day we still commemorate as a Festival of Sacrifice. When I was young, I stood in that arena in the Albert Hall. The shower of poppies was one of the most unnerving experiences I have ever had.

So, we have Hallowe'en or more correctly Samhaine. A fire rite, which we still celebrate as a fire rite, but on a different day, courtesy of seventeenth century Puritans. November 5th is the same rite, slightly moved in the calender, the spiritual connections of which are largely forgotten, or hidden.

The old people of England were not going to be cheated of their festival, and were quite happy to pretend to celebrate the unpleasant death of one Guido Fawkes, they liked a good execution. He tried to do what we all sometimes feel like. A nice piece of graffiti states, "Come back, Guy Fawkes, all is forgiven".

A great deal of staff work is required on the part of the person heading this rite. First, a site needs to be found where a large fire can be safely built. There should be a safe box for matches, fireworks, sparklers and rockets. An altar, possibly the trunk of a fallen tree or a large stone, for wine, (I like sloe gin for this rite;) and for oatcakes.

The removal of cowpats, thistles and nettles is a good idea, and puddles and rabbit holes avoided or filled in. If a script is necessary, and for a lot of old rites it shouldn't be, make sure that everyone has it long enough beforehand to know what they are doing and saying. It is hard to read by flickering candlelight, even if these are in lanterns and I do not like torches although I agree that sometimes they are necessary. Garden flares are fine, but often the wind is too strong for them and they go out. They were meant to be used in a garden on a warm summer evening.

When I first wrote this book I said that one should have a robe or cloak. Nowadays, for outside working, I prefer to recommend wellies and windproof anoraks or barbours. If you have a wool cloak by all means wear it, so long as you keep it away from the fire. But I still say that late October is no time to go about half-clothed and definitely not naked. Are you crazy?

Having done all this preparation, there will be a severe gale and the rain will come down in torrents and there is a strike. "I'm not going out in that." So you need an alternative which is usually the sitting room. This means getting rid of all the furniture, racing round with the vacuum cleaner, do you ALWAYS vacuum under YOUR sofa?

You must also make a secure place for dogs, cats and children. The first two you would naturally keep safe anyway, they do not like fireworks. This also means making sure you have the right kind of fireworks, unless you intend to brave the elements to let them off outside. I do not like children to attend the Samhaine rite. In fact, I have made myself vastly unpopular with those who wish to bring them. This rite is no place for small children. One should remember that they are much more psychic than adults and would probably see things which would frighten them.

If wet, indoors

A tiny fire in the cauldron, which is standing upon a suitable tile or brick and candles instead of flares. The mention of indoor fireworks is not funny. We had a nasty time one year when outdoor ones were used inside, we all nearly choked.

I cannot imagine why anyone should associate witches with the smell of sulphur, it is a most distressing smell. We usually smell of something nice, like Frankincense or Sandalwood,

Chypre or Number 5. My daughters-in-law prefer Poison or Opium.

Working indoors means a lot of nonsense about getting ready and I do wish I had another room. This, you understand, is an excuse to do the rite robed, so the men go into one tiny bedroom and the women into mine, which is usually enormously untidy, but some people prefer the kitchen and some the loo. When you wear a robe, do try not to wear all your everyday clothes underneath. You are putting on a different persona, another you, and sweaters and slacks are not really part of that. I don't say that you should always strip completely, but do use a bit of nous.

Outside, we do not raise a circle, we try to spread the work over the whole Island, to it's sea-girt boundaries, but for some reason people feel more comfortable with one indoors. We also put up conventional quarters, not with pentagrams but with spirals. These are not necessarily in the accepted places either, but are more likely to be where the elements actually are. If the wind is coming from the South-West, that is where Air is and so on. The rain will also be coming from that direction too, so choose for yourself. Do state the reason for the rite, which in this case includes the bi-annual punch-up between the Oak and the Holly. We have tried to make this a discussion between these two on the respective duties of the two halves of the same whole. This is, on the face of it, for me at least, an incredible bow to New Age conventions. I'm not sure I like it. The old way, of a few good blows exchanged while the discussion is taking place seems to bring home the whole idea better. The Holly and the Oak being respectively the Winter and Summer aspects of the Horned Lord, the Lady's consort. Each one is responsible to the other for the safety and wellbeing of the People during the other's absence in the Otherworld or the Greenwood, whichever you like to call it.

There is a very good reason why we leave the circle open. In the course of our long and rather bloody history, very few parts of the Island have escaped becoming a battlefield. We ask the wandering spirits to come to the rite and we offer them a doorway to their rest at the end of it.

This, we hope, will be their last ritual on this Earth Walk, as the North American Indians call it. I like that phrase. When we first did this, the area filled with people from every age and many passed through the fire. Now, not quite so many come. This is another good reason for prohibiting the presence of children. We each choose a tribe and called them to follow us:-

"Follow, Follow, and Find the Light.."

We jump over the fire and they pass through, the fire is a doorway opened at the beginning of the rite and of course, protected so that nothing can come out the other way.

This is the ending of the year. The Oak, His sap fallen to earth and his power gone, leaves the rite with the Lady. They go down into the Otherworld to rest until Spring. We dance a round dance, giving to the fire papers we have prepared with the things we wish to leave behind. The problems which have beset us and the friendships that have come apart. This is a solemn dance, widdershins round the fire.

When the dance has ended, we wait a few minutes to allow the papers to finish burning and then let off rockets and fireworks to welcome in the Lord of the Holly, who is also Herne the Hunter, who comes to protect us through the dark time of the year. Dry wood is thrown on the fire to make it blaze up, and we welcome Herne, who has quite a lot to say to us. When he is finished we dance a merry dance, waving sparklers and we pass small presents to one another. We drink our wine and eat our oatcakes, leaving crumbs for the birds and giving libations to the earth.

We go back into the circle and each one of us calls a group of people through the fire, Celt, Aborigine, Roman, Norman, Saxon. Man, woman and child. All who have died and have not gone back to the Mother, for whatever reason are called. One person will call on the souls of the Seamen who died on the convoys; another calls on the men who died in the Civil War, one even called on the souls of the German pilots who died during the Battle of Britain and the blitz. Including:-

"Those who fought at Tumbledown
Or died at Alamain."

All must go back eventually to the Mother.

We thank all who came and suggest that this is the time to go. I NEVER dismiss the quarters. I hope I am not that arrogant. They will go in their own good time.

We put the lights out and leave the circle or the site. We might have a feast after this, dressed in the clothes of those we called, but no-one comes dressed as a witch. As there has been quite a lot of dancing during the rite and it is cold, people have worked up an appetite.

The notion that baked potatoes, beans and sausages are a reasonable feast I find very poor. I like plenty of Punch and a good thick casserole, I like gilding the lily. I am apt to forget that some folk are vegetarians but they know this by now and bring plenty for themselves. Although one poor chap feasted on apples.

After the feast we play all the games associated with the season. Apple bobbing, both in water and with the apples hanging from the ceiling; grubbing for a penny in a mountain of flour and conkers. The games of this season are inclined to be mucky and if you play the flour game AFTER Apple Bobbing you can become glued to your clothes. It is as well to wear something old and washable, and probably bring a change of clothing.

Many of these games are connected with divination, usually to see one's future love or learn his name. Most people have played them at one time or another.

Apple Peeling

Peel an apple carefully, so that the peel stays in one long strip. Throw it over the left shoulder, (this is because most people are right handed). If it lands in one piece it is supposed to show the initial of one's true love.

Exploding Nuts

A couple each throw a nut onto the fire. If they explode, love is great. If they merely whimper, love is dying. If one does one thing and the other something else, draw your own conclusions.

Floating Oak Apples

This one tells how faithful you love is. Put two oak apples into a bowl of water. If they float together she/he is faithful. If they float apart - look for someone else.

Mutton Bones

You will naturally have a spare mutton bone about your person.

Two people are required for this, one of them with the 'sight'.

Scrape all the meat carefully from the bone using anything but metal, as this ruins the spell. A really sharp flint does the job well, or even better, leave it where flies can lay eggs on it. The maggots make it clean as a whistle. If you time this right, robins and wrens will feed on the maggots. O.K. Who said witchcraft was politically correct?

One person holds the bone over his left shoulder (the right handed thing again), and the other looks through the thinnest part of the broad end. If he has the 'sight' he should be able to "see" the answers to questions put to him by the group.

There were so many ways to see one's future spouse. In Oxfordshire, girls would climb over the walls of a churchyard, borrow the scythe and cut down the hempseed, not Cannabis, but more likely Hemp Nettle, *Galeopsis tetrahit*, and holding a bunch in her hand, peer into the shadows to see the shade of her husband-to-be. I'm not sure what they might do with a petrol grass cutter, and I'm sure hempseed is illegal.

In Cornwall, one might be given an "Allan" apple for good luck. Placed under a young girl's pillow, she might see her future husband - if she could sleep for the bump.

If you sit in a fairy ring on Samhaine Eve, the veil being thin, you might be whisked away entirely, never to be seen again. As I mentioned before, the old Samhaine day was November 11th, which is St, Martin's Day. Kingfishers brooding at that time brought a late and lovely summer.

You can place the ash from the Samhaine fire in your shoes for a lucky year.

A more gruesome foretelling is also to do with fire. Riddle the ashes as soon as the fire goes out, tip them onto the hearth and go to bed. If there is a footprint in the ash in the morning, the one whose shoe fits will not be long for this world.

Before going to bed, leave a feast for the departed.

X   X   X   X   X

It was the custom to let the fires go out at the end of the year and to re-light them from the embers of the Samhaine fire. This was not just a custom but in the times of the Druids was a law. One had to pay the Druid for the embers, one of his perks and ill luck it was to anyone who didn't play. This is often done now at New Year. It signifies a clearing out of old ideas and a taking in of new ones, making room for new knowledge coming in. The human brain is not used to its full capacity and the little bit we do use might easily get overloaded.

Witches are often accused of desecrating churches. Now this is something I do not understand. Why, when we prefer to worship out of doors, should churches bother us? Well, perhaps it is because many of the most ancient churches were deliberately built on our sacred sites. Our sacred wells were not only given the names of saints, I was most incensed when I discovered that the holy well under the hill at Cerne Abbas, had been dedicated to St. Austin, a corruption, I think, of Augustine. Why were they not, at least, given a woman's name? Oh, yes, the font, which is usually found close to the old North door of the older churches, was where the spring would have been on the sacred site. The North door was called the Devil's door. That was the way the old folk insisted upon entering the church, the way they had always entered the site.

However, it is not the church which interests witches but the SITE. So many of them are round, you see. I have this idea that a group of witches, looking for somewhere to hold a rite, especially in a town where aldermen and councillors, beadles, wardens and constables, not to mention Peeping Toms and nosy neighbours, would have found a churchyard quite tempting.

At Hallowe'en and Walpurgis night, these places are legendary, full of ghoolies and ghosties and long leggety beasties, all smelling of decay and wailing and glowing in the dark.

Now, put yourself in the witch's shoes. Here is a place where few people would go, not even the Watch. So, gild the lily, make it really scary. If they expect the dead to rise from the grave, let it happen. Have your young people dress in rags which have been smeared with rotten fish. These would not only glow but stink like hell. This is what the populace expect. Teach your young to rise from behind the tombstones and out of the steps of the mausoleums, wailing and going 'wooooo' a lot. Not many hardy citizens would venture into the churchyard after midnight, and the rite could go ahead unmolested. To our modern minds, the very idea of wearing such garments would be nauseating, but our forebears were not so nice.

The West Wind Sabbat

Another name for this festival is the West Wind Sabbat and the moon is the Elder Tree Moon. This is only to be expected as the Elder is seen as the embodiment of the Crone and the West is Her quarter. This is the third phase of the Goddess.

One must always be very polite to the Elder and one must ask before taking anything from Her, whether it be blossom, berries or bark. If I collect flowers in Spring for wine or for Elder Flower Water, which is good for the complexion, I always say *"Madam, may I take your flowers for my use?"* I then wait, and it often seems that I am shown which blossoms I may cut. In the Autumn when the tree is full of berries, I go again to the tree, this time asking *"Madam, may I have some berries for a potion. We humans suffer from coughs and sore throats and your fruit can soothe us."* I've never been refused yet. This recipe has been published in several books and it is more or less as my granny made it.

Take several pounds of very ripe elderberries. Strip them from the twigs with a fork and put them in a covered pan, (with no added water), place into an oven on a very low heat. Let them sweat for several hours, overnight is best. Next day, drain off the juice and mix with honey, warming until the honey has melted. DO NOT BOIL. or you will destroy the very volatile Vitamin C. If you have a little rum or some whisky, this will help the mixture to keep, but it isn't really necessary. It is quite delicious as it is. Pour melted wax into the neck of the bottle and it should keep for several months. Take two or three spoonsful, or a tablespoonful in hot, not boiling water, when you have a cold or sore throat. It will do wonders. When drinking it you should say:-

> *"Madam, I drink this potion off*
> *To cure my rather nasty cough."*

Every part of the Elder is good for something. Dyes were made from the bark, leaves and berries. The bark makes a black dye, the leaves green, with the proper mordant, and the berries blue or indigo. Every part of the tree can be usefully employed, including the inner bark and the first green shoots.

Remember, when you take something from the Elder, always seek permission. *"Auld Gal, Gimme some o' thi' wood, and I'll gi' thee some o' mine when I grow into a tree."* It is also a good idea to give something on account. On account of, if you don't, She might get annoyed. Take a bottle of mixed honey, grain and water, and sprinkle some over her roots.

To Pickle Elder Buds

"Boil water and salt together, put in the buds and let them boil a while but not until they are tender. Strain and set to cool. In the meantime boil White Wine Vinegar with two blades of mace and a little whole pepper. Put in the buds and let them stand for nine days. Scald them in a brass pan six or seven times until they are as green as grass, but take care they do not get soft. Put into pots and tie down with leather." There would probably be some E. U. restriction upon doing this. It is possibly unhygenic, or unacceptable to our reluctant European brethren. Better use an ordinary jam pot cover.

Culpeper, upon whom I dote, says:-

"The first shoots of the common Elder boiled like asparagus, and the young leaves and shoots boiled in a fat broth, do mightily carry off phlegm and cholor." I thought you'd like to know that.

John Evelyn said:-

"If the medicinal properties of the leaves, bark, berries etc. were thoroughly known, I cannot tell what our countrymen would ail, for which they might not find a remedy..."

Elderberry wine looks and tastes like rich, ruby port and was often used to dilute the same by the unscrupulous dealers of the nineteenth century. Like that, it probably did not cause the gout, and was used to sweat out fevers.

We used to scoop out the pith from the wood to make musical pipes when I was young. Of these Pliny says *"Countrymen believe that the most sonorous horns were made of elder which had never heard the cock crow."*

Never, never try to burn the wood. "T'awd Gal Down"t like it." It spits like blazes and can start many a fire. The name comes from the Anglo-Saxon *"Aeld"* meaning Fire and the hollow branches were used to blow up the flames. The generic name *Sambucus* was used by Pliny and is derived from the Greek *sambuca*, referring to the Roman musical instrument.

The pith was often used by botanists to hold a small specimen steady while they sliced them.

The blossoms, besides making the extremely elegant Elderflower champagne, (oops sorry, we are not allowed to say that, are we?).

make an absolutely gorgeous early summer pudding. Elderflower fritters, which I will tell you about when we come to Beltaine.

The Elder is magic in whichever part of the world you find it, Forget about the legend of Judas hanging himself. The branches are not strong enough to hold a heavy body, they would split and the most he would have done was stretch his neck a bit and probably break a leg.

The Elder Queen, mother of elves, lived in the roots, which is why, oh, my best beloved, you do not cut the tree about without permission. You Can, on January 6th, (although whether this is Julian or Gregorian I can't say), ask permission and cut a branch, (you have to spit three times if this is not given). You make a circle with the branch in a lonely place and if you have a deep desire to be both invisible and probably zapped, you can demand? of the Devil some of his precious fern seed that gives the possessor the strength of thirty men. (It also keeps worms out of furniture, fends off snakes and cures toothache.) I would rather be conspicuous than try this. you would have to be several bricks short of a building set to do it.

Culpeper also says "*it is needless to write any description of it since any boy that plays with a pop-gun will not mistake another tree for an elder.*" The same cannot be said for publishers. In the rather more colourful first edition of this book, published some years ago, I had specified an elder and was startled to be given a picture of a rowan instead.

There is a country belief that, if the flowers are put into ale, and a man and woman drink it together, they will be married within a year.

Thyme   *Thymus Vulgaris*

Thyme is associated with the souls of the departed so should be included in incenses made for Samhaine. Rosemary is for remembrance and it would be well to include Deadly Nightshade for this aids astral projection.

There are so many types of thyme now, I once tried to get a specimen of every kind available but gave up after twenty four.

"Thyme for the time it lasteth,
Yieldeth most honie and
  therefore
in old Time, was counted
  Chief." Anon.

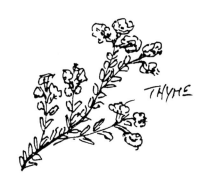

THYME

Honey bees love it and that which comes from bees exclusively farming thyme blossom is really delicious. It was long revered as a symbol for bravery. I wonder why those people afflicted with shyness or bashfulness do not drink a soup made from beer and thyme. In the seventeenth century it was considered to be a sovereign cure for both these problems.

It does well on very poor well-drained soil, which is why it smells so strong in Greece. The islands I am told, are redolent of this herb.

Deadly Nightshade

Culpeper says that the leaves and part of the root may be used as a poultice for inflammatory swellings. The leaves, placed over lumps in the breast, relieves and dissipates them. The swellings, not the breasts. Never, on any account take this herb internally, especially after reading this book. I have no wish to explain myself to a magistrate. The dried leaves and flowers might be added to incense to open up the psyche. It was an ingredient of "Flying Ointment." I have never been convinced that witches could fly on broomsticks, stalks of ragwort or even hurdles. The ointment, made from various hallucinogens, and rubbed on the body, which no doubt brought them out in a nasty rash, might very well send one on a trip and one might think one was flying.

It is a shame to explode such old saws I know, but my broomstick has never budged, even when I leave it out in the full moon to charge it up and chant..."*Tragona Macoides, Tracorum Satus Dea*"

It is very good for sweeping up leaves though.

Coming at the end of Autumn, closely followed by the first day of Winter, November 1st, Samhaine is firmly in Scorpio, which according to Astrology is the House of Death. It is ruled by Pluto, the God of the Underworld, the Roman version of the Druid's Dis. Pluto governs life and death, which should be self-evident. Throughout Scorpio we have to face the consequences of any actions taken during the year. Any issues ducked annually, at Samhaine will need to be faced at ultimate death, and then you will be least able to cope. So sort yourself out and then think of the things you wish to keep in your life. Think of new friendships, new learnings and how you will make time for them in the year to come. This really is the forerunner of making New Year's Resolutions.

Before Pluto was discovered, the governing planet was Saturn, who a great friend of mine says "*Shows the unforgiving loveliness of wisdom.*"

A Spell for Samhaine Eve

The Yew is great in age and girth
A symbol of both death and birth.
Endings and beginnings it will spin
At Samhaine, when the veil is thin.

Three times round it's girth we tread
Releasing mourners from their dread.

A knife to cut the spirit free
From bonds imposed by family
A bow to make the spirit fly
To Resurrection, by and by.

A sprig for mourners all we take
To give them peace for their own sake.

A Chant for Samhaine Eve

The Lord is Holly and is Oak
Two sides in one - so say our folk.
The Oak Lord goes - the Holly stays
To help us through the winter days.

Carol for Samhaine

Elder, Birch and Oak may go,
Yew and Holly stay,
To see the Craft through winter chill
To joyous May.

A twig with three or four knots, which has been dedicated to either the God or the Goddess was carried as a talisman to ward off rheumatism.

In the days when hedges were properly layed, instead of being torn out, the hedgers were allowed to take home faggots for their fires, but however much elder wood was left, they wouldn't take that. Farmers will not drive cattle with elder sticks and their wives will not use it for skewers for dressing poultry, another thing most of us do not do now, it is a lost art.

The Swan

This beautiful bird was often considered to be a bird of ill-omen unless you met one on a warm Friday afternoon. Swan maidens

lured young men to watery graves. There was a Celtic princess called Caer Obonmeith who, with all her maidens, turned into a swan on the Eve of Samhaine and called pitifully until the young men of the village came, then they beckoned them into the lake and drowned them. I'm sure she was a very nice girl most of the time, she couldn't help being bewitched.

It was extremely unlucky to kill a swan because they are said to embody human souls. They are much more faithful than humans, they really do mate for life and it is really tragic to see a swan whose mate has died. They mourn, and sometimes will not mate again.

Apollo's chariot was drawn by swans when he flew to the Land of Youth, beyond the North Wind.

There is an old superstition that the eggs hatch only during storms and that the thunder and lightning break the shells.

They not only sing when they die, according to Irish legend. A great company alighted on Lough Bel Dragon, wearing silver chains and golden crowns. They sang so sweetly that all who heard them fell asleep for three nights and days.

Turquoise

Although I know very little about the Egyptians, I do know something about Chaldeans, who associated this stone with their version of Saturn. It represents strength and power and is a night time jewel. It was "the breath of spirit and life."

It represents beauty and the Egyptians carved it into the shape of the lotus but the Chaldeans discovered how to make cloisonne jewellery which was golden shapes patterned with soldered wires, the shapes filled in with turquoise, which imitated the lotus leaf. Far more exacting than merely carving the stone.

It was the royal jewel of the Persian kings who used it to protect their horses. It came to Europe from Turkey, hence it's name, possibly with the return of the crusaders, in the fourteenth century.

In the fourteenth century it was used to protect horses from the ill effects of drinking cold water when they had been racing. Anyone who gives a horse cold water, in these circumstances should, in my opinion, be shot.

In the Seventeenth century it was worn only by men. The idea of strength and power, I suppose.

North American shamans wore this jewel a great deal, I am not sure if the women are allowed to wear it. Their Braves carried a piece with them into battle because it gave them courage.

Because of its high copper content it is an especially good conductor for healing and is considered to be good for both rheumatism and arthritis.

It is a good colour to wear if you have to address a meeting or a group especially if you can wear it near the throat.

Chapter Two

THE WINTER SOLSTICE

December 21st

"The rising of the Sun and the Running of the Deer."

This is the rite everyone likes, because not only have we *"Decked the hall with boughs of Holly"* nor because we always have a glorious feast after the rite but because of that very special feeling abroad at this time of the year. I was born in Kent, a county noted, at that time, for its very cold winters and I would be prepared to bet quite a lot of money that our Christmases were always white. I especially loved the shops with their pomegranates and oranges which were then available only in the winter.

The chill of the greengrocers and the smell of all that lovely, bright fruit seen through the lighted windows began the season for me.

It might seem strange for a witch to say that she enjoyed carol singing, but like most things, we had 'em first. 'To carol', is to sing in a round; alternatively, a ring dance performed while singing. Most people now know the original words of the carols, although I must admit to singing "*Away in a manger*" quite happily. We had a harmonium on the trailer or the wagon if my grandfather would let us have the horse. I felt like the field mice in the "*Wind in the Willows*" "*Red worsted mufflers round their throats, forepaws dug deep into their pockets, their feet jiggling for warmth.*"

I suppose that I believed what I sang at the time and in many ways it is true. There was always a miraculous child born at Midwinter, Jesus was only one of them. All the others were pagan and Jesus was more probably born in the spring, but this cannot take away the magic of the time.

We do most of the things Christians do and we did them first. We decorate the house with as much greenery as we can, we give presents and we have a wonderful time. We once had a Medieval banquet after the rite, but note the word 'once'. Having cooked nine courses for eighteen people, all dressed up in their best fancy dress, the only thing I could be was the kitchen drudge. Never again. But one should try everything once.

I have to prepare for three festivals, the Solstice, my annual party and Christmas for my grandchildren. I need to begin early. I spend weeks before, preparing food, including some extremely alcoholic trifles, which my mother called "Tipsy Cake" and when I tell you that I begin them four days before the rite, by soaking the fruit in brandy and the sponge cakes in sherry, and that each succeeding ingredient is well anointed with booze you will see why.

Then I collect as much holly as I can beg from acquaintances and bags full of long trailing ivy. Sometimes, if I have help, we bring in some ivy-covered trunks to stand in the corners of the room. I know a few places where mistletoe grows in profusion and lastly a few boughs of pine or fir.

Then comes the organisation. I get the working party cleaning the house and moving furniture. We run a whole web of strings from one corner of the room to the other. The centre lampshade must be removed to give room for the mistletoe ball. I sometimes wonder how I keep my friends.

We cover the bookshelves with white sheets and those with "snow' and fir boughs. the strings are wound with ivy and holly and sometimes a little tinsel and the scene is set. This is for the indoor rite you will understand. There are times when we work outside, but it is usually far too cold, although my group are a hardy lot and prefer to be out of doors if this is at all possible.

There is nowhere to sit and everyone is already shattered. We must have supper and showers and make some room for the rest of the group, who turn up just in time for supper. Luckily, they are all well trained and head straight for the kitchen, adding their contributions to the later feast. I have a large bowl of mulled wine simmering on the stove and someone shouts that they can't find the glasses. As they have been in the same cupboard for many years I shout back that they are where they usually are. But the cupboard has been hidden behind a sheet.

When everyone has drunk a cup or so of punch, and washed their glass, they go upstairs to change, leaving me to make some changes of mine own. That is changing a very ordinary living room into a magical temple. The Ivy-clad ceiling and the bunches of green help to foster the concept of a snow filled glade deep in a wood. The smell of the newly cut pine and the holly intensify this. After a final vacuuming, candles and incense are lit and we are ready to go.

This is one rite in which we have priestesses, and even the odd priest. Note, this is NOT a High priest. As we have no initiation we have no hierarchy but everyone who takes part in such a rite is in their way, a priest or priestess. One man either represents Herne, or calls HIM when we use a disembodied voice backed by the wailing of the wind and tossing trees.

We need a piper or Jack-in-the-Green, and someone to bang a drum and the four people to call the Quarters. This is about the only way that we march in step with other magical groups.

We have developed a rite over the years which has a large number of speaking parts. Herne is Lord of the greenwood and we include many animals in the rite. The Owl, Raven, Heron, Kingfisher, Eagle and Pheasant. A Badger, a Salmon and a Wolf. Sometimes a Dog and a Horse if enough people are present. There must be a Robin and a Wren, for the Hunting, and a Priestess of the Barley. The quarters are called Priests of Dawn and Midday, and the Priestesses Twilight and Midnight.

We also need a Man and a Woman to take instruction and to ask questions.

The Winter Solstice Rite

The Priestess of Midnight stands alone in the glade. She lights a very large red candle, which stands in a cauldron surrounded by the best holly, ivy and mistletoe. When she feels that the atmosphere has stilled, she  takes up a temple singing bowl and runs a mahogany rod round the edge. A strange belling noise reverberates through the glade and Jack-in-the-Green and the drummer come in, sit down and begin to play.

On hearing the music, the group approaches the door, where a Watchman stands holding a bowl of hyssop scented water and a clean towel. He has a small branch of hyssop with which he sprinkles water on each person, and each one rinses their fingers in the bowl and dries their hands. This is to signify cleansing before entering the glade.

As they enter, they circle three times
sunwise, or deosil, pronounced "jessil".

The Priestess of Midnight has moved
outside the circle, Herne has taken up a
position opposite her also outside the
circle.

The Priestess speaks:-

> *"I am the raven, Lady of the
> Underworld, Dread Persephone,
> Goddess of Life, Death and Re-birth. I am
> She who Was, Is and Will Be. The Goddess
> facing Both Ways. MORRIGAN.*

> *At this time I return from my dream realm
> to learn how my children have fared since
> Samhaine. The wheel of thirteen spokes
> has returned to Midwinter.*

> *On this, the darkest night of the
> year, we meet once more to enact
> the old traditions; to renew our
> faith and our trust; and to meet
> with our Lord Herne. I come to see
> how well you celebrate and under-
> stand the turning of the wheel and to
> greet My Lord of the Holly, the Dark
> Lord, the Lord of Winter, Herne the
> Hunter. He who hunts my hounds
> through the dark clear spaces of the
> night.*

> *I greet my Lord and Consort. How fare you,
> Lord Herne?"*

Herne speaks:-

> *"Greetings, My Lady. We have missed you in the time you
> have been in the Underworld. Our Children are well and
> keep faith, as you see.*
>
> *Greetings, My Children. I am the Dark Hunter and the
> Hounds I hunt are the Yell Hounds, the Hounds of Helle, the
> Goddess's own pack. We hunt those who have damaged the
> Land; those who have transgressed against the laws of
> Nature; So you who keep faith have no need to fear.*
>
> *At this time of deepest winter when darkness enfolds the
> Land, I am with you. I will lead you through the deep night
> when the icy wind from the Northern mountains blows most
> strongly and the frost and snow makes the ground hard.
> Remember your smaller, four-footed brethren, the cold is
> harder for them. Feed them where you can and remember,
> they need water as well as food."*

He turns back to the Priestess.

> *"Welcome Lady, this darkest night. It is an unlooked-for
> blessing to see you again. Even you, My Children, cannot
> know what this means to me."*

The Priestess of Midnight speaks:-

> *"I thank you, My Lord. I am the Raven, Goddess Facing
> Both Ways. I am called Arianrhod of the Silver wheel,
> turning and turning through space, changing the seasons,
> changing the times of Light and Darkness. I am called
> Kerridwen of the Cauldron and here we have Three
> Cauldrons, each has its own use, each a Cauldron of
> Inspiration."*

She begins to move into the circle, spiralling into the centre.

"*I come from the realms of Darkness and Dreaming for just a short time until I return again in spring. I bring with me the Light of Re-birth and this is my gift to you at this Solstice. The days have been dark since Samhaine, sometimes the fog has been so grey that no light could be seen. Much of winter is yet to come but you are in the safe hands of Herne, who will guard you. So be of good cheer and fear not. This light is a Symbol of the Light to come.*"

She lights the centre candle on the altar with the words:-

"*As the Dawn brings the light of a new day, a small light which will grow, I light the candle that others may increase the light. Come, My Children, and join the rite.*"

The Raven leaves the circle and goes back to the North.

The Officers call the Quarters.

We call "*Those who dwell in the N. S. E. & W.*" and their archetypes and totems." We do not call kings, elementals or angels. We are witches, not magicians.

In the South West, and the South East, a series of sighting posts have been set to mark the time of the solstice. You can see these at any stone circle, if you look hard enough.

The Priestess of Twilight leads the Man and the Woman to the sighting posts of the South West. She speaks:-

"Long ago, in the dreamtime of our race, a man and a woman kept watch as the sun set in winter. They looked for the beginning of the longest night. They placed a stone on yonder hill and another here, just outside the village. At this time we watch as did our fathers' fathers and we see how straight the line is between these two posts and the setting sun.

This is the first of the mysteries you will learn this night.

When you have seen, go and tell the people that tonight is the longest of the year and the wheel spins. Thus the tribe will know that this is a special time and in three days from now, when the Sun begins His journey back from the South, Midwinter Eve will have come again and they may rejoice."

She returns to her place and the Man and the Woman go round the circle telling everyone what they have seen. When they have shared the mystery they return to their places.

At this point the Priestess of the Barley takes a wooden bowl of ears of barley round the circle. Each person takes an ear and the priestess instructs them to rub the grain between their fingers, separating the seed from the chaff into which they must put all the problems and disappointments of the past year. She takes another bowl round the circle collecting the chaff. She tells them that this

will be burned upon the fire and she does this when she returns to the altar.

A drum will beat all begin a slow, circling movement widdershins, thinking of all they have thrown away.

She then tells them to put into the seed all the ideas and hopes they wish to grow in the coming year and that after the Night of the Plough these will be broadcast over the field to grow with the farmer's grain. This barley has been taken from the field and it is well that it should be returned. This ensures yet another loop of the spiral of life. She takes the bowl round the circle and collects the grain from each person.

When this is completed and the chaff has been burned the drum beats again, Jack in the Green will play a merry tune and we dance the weaving dance, men facing right and women left as has been previously described. This is to weave into our lives all those things we have given into the care of the seed.

The Priestess of Fire says:-

> "Our Lady of the Earth now dwells in the fairie realms of the Otherworld until Her time of re-birth. Have no fear, for though She has gone from us She only sleeps, coming in dreams to us when we need Her. She has given us a token of new Light and Life. From this token I light the fire of the Sun to give Him strength to return as the wheel turns."

She walks to the southern cauldron and with a flame from the great candle she kindles the fire.

> "We must all give something back to the Goddess. We have given our woes and dreams. Let us offer something to the coming Light."

She takes a lantern round the circle, pausing at each person and asks:-

> "What will you give to the coming Light?"

45

Each one has been given the name of a bird or animal and answers:-

EAGLE

"I will give the sweep of my wings and the chill soaring heights of Air. I see far into the Otherworld. I am a champion. All my strength I will give that the seasons may turn."

The priestess lights his candle.

PHEASANT

"I will give the flesh of my body and the wild beauty of the forest margins. I am golden fronted. I sustain. All my strength I will give that the seasons may turn."

KINGFISHER

"I will give the blue lightning of my flight and the sweet swiftness of clear rivers. I am a dancer. I please the eye. All my strength I will give that the seasons may turn."

The priestess goes round the circle and lights each candle after the offering. Each one repeats the *"All my strength..."* after their own gift.

RAVEN *I will give the carrion feast, the Night of Truth. I see that all things die and are re-born. I am a winnower. I am a magician. All my strength...."*

HERON *"I will give the hearth and home. I make my nest in the treetops. I am a lover. I am a deliverer. Etc."*

SALMON *"I give the paths of the seas and the stillness of lakes. I am a bard. I am the Oldest One.*

BADGER *'I give the deep places of earth, the holts and the homes. I am a warrior. I am a maker."*

OWL

"It is well, for if a single one of you withholds the smallest part the long night will fall upon us and the Sun will not return in splendour. I give the wisdom of the darkness of unforgiving night and the eyes to see the path. All my strength I will give that the seasons may turn."

HERNE

'It is well. I give my body and skin, my hooves and horns. I give the wild woods and the lonely heath. I am a King. I am a teacher. All my strength I will give............"

P. of Fire

"Each has given freely, and in three days the world will awake to the birth of the Unconquered Sun. As the sun rises and sets, give back to the Land what you have taken and it will give freely to you."

There should be a magical creature for everyone present, and the words can be easily thought of. End each giving with the words *"all my strength I will give...."*

The next part of the rite is the Hunting of the Wren. This is a very ancient tradition symbolising the end and the beginning of the yearly cycle. The Wren is the Old year which has to die that the wheel may turn. The Robin is the New year. The "Hunting" usually happens on the evening of the calender New Year nowadays, but was originally done on the Solstice.

Before the Hunt can take place, the Wren tells her story.

> *"I am the Wren, Arianrhod of the Silver Wheel, smallest of Birds. Yet I was carried on the back of the Eagle and when He could go no higher, I flew off and so carried the palm. I am the Old Year. This night I must die that the season may turn, but only if my son, the Robin can kill me."*

The Robin must prove his worth and his right to hunt and he does this by answering three riddles.

PHEASANT   'Why am I the head of the Consonants?"

ROBIN   *"As the Stag is the best of flesh that runs, so the pheasant is the best that flies."*

WREN   *"Why am I in the central place?"*

ROBIN   'The Oak is the King of the Trees, the Wren
                          is the King of Birds. The Wren is the Soul
                          of the Oak."

RAVEN   *"Why am I in the last place?"*

ROBIN   *"The Raven wears mourning for the King*
                          who dies this night."

The Owl and Herne both say: *"Well answered. Where may he be struck?"*

The Robin replies, *"Between the sinew and the bone of His right leg."*

The Hunt begins. All sing the *Cutty Wren*. The first verse is well known, beginning *"Where are you going? said Milder to Molder. "We may not tell you" said Festle to Fose, "We're hunting the Wren, said Johnny Red Nose. Hunting the Wren Said everyone."*

There are several verses to this and between each verse, which should be sung by the men, the women sing:-

> *"Round and round and round again,*
> *They hunt, they hunt to catch the Wren."*

After the last verse they all sing:

> *"We hunted the Wren for Robbin the Bobbin.*
> *We hunted the Wren for Jack in the Green.*
> *We hunted the Wren for Robbin the Bobbin.*
> *We hunted the Wren for everyone."*

Up to this moment, the Wren has been sitting upon a golden crown, decorated with holly, ivy and mistletoe, but now she is taken off and placed in a glass case lined with ivy. The Robin takes her place on the crown. These are symbolic birds, you

50

understand. Do not try to get real ones. Ours are made from pottery.

At this point the Priestesses of Fire and Barley take the cup of mead and the pieces of fruit cake round the circle, wishing everyone a Happy Solstice and all the compliments of the season. I said in the last chapter that we did not have priestesses to do this. This rite, however, is an exception.

A kiss should be exchanged as the mead and cake are offered. The circle should break up and everyone should embrace one another and any gifts exchanged. This should take a few minutes, giving time to relax a little before the pathworking, which is a long one. If anyone requires a chair, this is a good time to get one. The cup should be passed many times and filled as necessary. When everyone is ready, take a seat and relax ready to take a journey through the year. Make yourselves comfortable and if you have a cloak, wear it. The path is long and one can get very cold.

The Journey Through the Year

The Sanctuary in the Woods

You have come to meet your friends in an ancient inn. The snow is deep and the wind is howling and you are glad to open the door. A great fire roars in the vast inglenook fireplace, a yule log of immense proportions.

Your friends greet you and mine host offers you mulled ale or wine and a large bowl of frumenty. There are piles of mince pies on wooden platters on the oak tables and you join one group. They ask how you fared on your journey to the inn and remind you, laughingly, not to drink too much. You all have far to go this night.

Look around you at the brightness of the holly berries and the mistletoe, which decorate the beams of the inn. You ask mine host how he came to find such fine branches, for the crop has been poor this year. He laughs and tells you that you will find some for yourself at the end of your journey.

Someone says that it is time to go, and you all shiver at the thought of going out into the blizzard. But you have promises to keep and go you must. Your friends drain their cups and finish off the mince pies. You all shrug into your cloaks and mine host opens a door which you remember from another time.

A flight of stairs goes down but not to a cellar. It leads to a passage of worked stone with a smooth flagged floor. Soon, however, the walls and floor get rougher and you must mind your steps. Before you is a pale light, coming from an opening at the end of the passage. The air strikes chill and you draw the hood of your cloak closer about your head.

You step out into a chill morning, just before dawn. It is difficult to see at first, but your eyes become accustomed to the light and the dawn is not far off. Look around you. You are in a dark wood. The snow has stopped but is piled round the boles of the trees, their boughs bending under the weight. The undergrowth is completely hidden, forming huge humps, which might provide cover for small animals.

As the light increases the snow begins to fade away, not melting exactly, but leaving a soft earthen smell. The ground beneath your boots is not muddy, as you might expect, but quite firm. You notice how lovely the wood is, filled with a deep peace. Snowdrops form a carpet beside a little river which chuckles over stones beneath a narrow bridge. Try not to step upon them.

Silver birches and rowans are just coming into leaf, while the new green shoots of honeysuckle and briar are unfolding. All around you now is the sound of birdsong and as you look along the stream you see a jewelled flash of colour, a kingfisher has come to bid you welcome.

Cross the bridge and you will find a path. On each side are stones covered with lichens the colours of jade, coral and amber. Cushions of moss show brilliant green and soon you will see primroses, smelling of warm honey, violets and wood anemonies. To your left is a marshy place where willow shoots show golden in shafts of sunlight. An alder, the tree of Bran, grows with its roots

53

practically in the water, it still has it's black cones from last year. Your path leads you through what seems like an old orchard of bent apple trees, showing blossom of pink and white. Blackthorns are in bloom too, for the brave blackthorn has blossoms before leaves.

The morning progresses. Small oaks are losing last years leaves as the buds of the new life start to show. Hawthorn boughs will soon be laden with blossom and further on there is a foam of elder flowers. The ash is rapidly putting on its leaves, and you can hear small creatures scurrying about their business but you cannot see them yet. Birdsong and the rustle of wings fill the air. You stop as you hear the hard, rapid tapping of a woodpecker finding grubs for its young. One of your companions points to an old stump and there is a lovely bird, black, white and red. She is not bothered by you. All the bustle only intensifies the stillness and peace that surrounds you.

Nearly all the trees are in full leaf now, only the oak stays, waiting for the May. It will soon be noon and some of the bustle dies away. The birds and the small animals are resting.

The path leads upward. The wood changes character. You are walking under great beeches, their delicate branches making the most delicate tracery in nature and you remember that the naves of the great cathedrals were built to imitate them.

A magnificent old oak, its new spring leaves tipped with scarlet, stands at the top of a

54

bank. You feel that you must pay your respects to this ancient sentinel of the wood. Here, you feel protected from harm, for the oak was called "the armour of the House of the Forest" by those who fled from persecution. Somewhere ahead you hear a clear, high piping - a liquid melody of incredible beauty. You know you must follow but by now it is midday and you are very thirsty.

A little way on there is the sound of falling water, and there it is, coming from a crack in a rock and falling into an obsidian bowl, worn smooth by centuries of the falling torrent. As the water overflows the bowl it begins a crystal clear brook banked by cresses, mints and bog myrtle. Look, there is a little frog sitting on a leaf. Beside the bowl is a small ledge upon which stands a finely chased silver cup. Above the ledge the legend "Drink well, traveller. Quench your thirst" is carved. You know that the water is safe to drink and after filling the cup you drink the sweetest water you have ever tasted. You splash your face and wrists with the overflowing water and take off your shoes and socks to paddle in the pool. You sit on the bank to rest for a few minutes before replacing your footwear. Have another drink from the spring and then cross the stream by some ancient stepping stones which have been worn smooth by the feet of many travellers, so take care.

The sound of piping merges with the song of thrush and blackbird. You scramble up the bank to an archway of thorns. Go through carefully, each holding stray branches for the others to pass under. Here the wood changes again and you are in mixed woodland. Graceful birches, rowans with their berries beginning to set. A few small hollies, their sweet blossom scenting the air. See the bright blue sky through the branches, for this is hot, high summer. Look, a jay - blue, buff with black and white striped wings, speeding past about it's affairs. It is said that our ancient oak forests were planted by the jay. The hollies stand out dark green even now. You notice that many animals are visible and they are all going your way; following the pipes.

The hot afternoon fades into evening and the trees take on their glorious autumn colours. High overhead in the canopy a nightingale begins his evening hymn. A pair of ashes stand like pillars on either side of the path and as you pass between them the wood again changes character. The trees are closer together, the piping has stopped and stillness deepens. Sycamores have turned gold and through a gathering mist a gold and silver birch gleams like a lantern.

A large white owl glides silently by, seeming to lead you on. A pair of stoats, their bright brown coats turning into winter white, and the black tips of their tails standing out clearly, (for the stoat is an ermine in winter) dance and play in front of you. They stand up on their tails to say "Hurry up" their bright eyes seeming to laugh at your slowness. The wind gets up and the leaves race by. You all catch as many as you can, for every leaf caught means a happy month to come. The wind dies down again with the last of the leaves, leaving you in gathering twilight among the bare trees in stillness.

Suddenly, this stillness is shattered by a raging bellow and the sound of clashing horns. The rut has begun and the stags are competing for the leadership of the hinds. You go along slowly now, and then, by a tree stump covered in bright moss you see a patch of wet soil and someone points out a dainty hoofprint, a fairy foot. You all look at it entranced for several minutes. Then, quite suddenly the piping begins again, very close now. Rabbits, mice, weasels and hedgehogs run past you, eagerly passing towards the sound of the music.

Overhead, squirrels, red and grey; pine martins and polecats leap through the branches. A constant stream of birds, robins, wrens, finches and tits is moving the same way. Right overhead a great heron flaps lazily. A badger and a fox trot along the path and all disappear beneath a solid looking wall of bramble and hawthorn. They still wear their leaves of bright jewel colours and have a few berries for the small creatures. You notice that the creatures of the wood have made for a smallish hole at the base of the barrier and as you hesitate, the owl comes to light on a branch and hoots at you. You know that you too can get through the hole, it is as big or as small as those who wish to use it.

Under the hedge it is dark and prickly and very earthy smelling but you push on and roll out the other side to find yourself in

FOX

RABBIT

SQUIRREL

dark, midwinter midnight. Snow lies deep, hard and crisp upon the ground and above you suddenly is a great, white moon. All about you are gigantic hollies and some unearthly light shows up the berries, and you know where the landlord of the inn found his solstice decorations. Yew trees make a hidden place in the centre of this sanctuary and standing beside an ancient stone, which looks like an altar, is the Great Horned Lord.

His eyes are deep and mysterious, yet full of love and humour. His features are chiselled and upon His brow are the magnificent antlers of a seven-tined stag. This is the Lord of the Wild Wood. For a moment, His horns change, becoming the delicate sweep of the goat horns of Pan, who holds the pipes between His fingers. The pipes which have been calling you

57

through the wood and the year, as they have called all the woodland creatures. He is the Friend and Protector of all His smaller brethren. His horns change back to antlers, for the Lords of the Wild Wood are one and they keep faith with all their subjects. This is the Holly Lord, who will see us safely through the winter. HERNE THE HUNTER.

About Him are the hounds, at peace and lying quietly, looking up at their Lord with love and obedience. Look carefully. Curled up between the paws of one is a small rabbit, quite unafraid. A wren perches on the head of another and a robin looks up expectantly. These are the fearsome Hounds of Hell, but the small creatures are not at all worried by their dread reputation.

Herne has been looking at the wounded paw of a hare and now He attends to a young buck, which has been injured by some careless huntsman. He looks up at this strange group of humans and His eyes are sad. He tends to the hurts of many small creatures and then he beckons us forward with a smile.

This is what we have come for but we all hesitate to approach. One who knows us for what we are. He waits and we dare to go to Him. The wind has been singing in the tops of the trees but now it dies down. He begins to speak. What He says is personal to each one of us but what He says fills us with awe and wonder. When He has spoken, we each offer our love and our service, repeating the oath we made at Samhaine. He smiles at each one of us, and blesses us.

As His words die away the piping begins once more and the trees seem to be singing an anthem of praise in which we all join. Our voices and the songs of the birds join with the wind as it softly stirs the branches.

You begin to feel sleepy.

Suddenly an owl hoots and you wake to find yourself sitting beneath the sentinel oak. The owl hoots once more and flies away. In the moonlight you can smell the scent of fir and pine, chilled by frost. And looking back into the shadows of the deep wood, something with horns moves majestically away.

You stand and find yourself outside the passage through which you entered into the wood. Go along it and find your door. Open it, go through and lock it and put the key away until another time.

You have been given an aspect of the Horned Lord to think about. Try to keep what He said to you in your heart and try to come to understand all that you saw and heard.

When you are ready, return and remember. There is a blessing on those who serve.

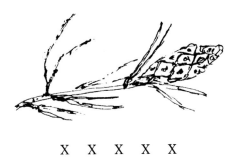

X   X   X   X   X

After the pathworking, our own piper plays a soft melody until we are all safely back. Then all stand.

The Priestess takes up the cauldron with the great red candle. She beckons to the Officer of the Dawn, who re-lights his candle and returns to his place. Each one in the circle comes to do the same thing and some light a second candle for someone they particularly wish to remember. When the circle re-forms we do another weaving dance and sing *"The Holly and the Ivy"* a very ancient pagan song. In time gone by, a carol was a song sung to a dance. Following the dance another cup of mead is passed round and we say:-

> *"Hail to the Returning sun.*
> *We drink to the Old Gods.*
> *To the Holly, and the Oak and the Lady.*
> *A merry Yule to all."*

Then we turn to the North and the officers close their quarters, extinguishing their candles as they finish. We offer thanks to all who have come to the rite. Finally, the priestess closes the circle saying *"The rite is ended. There is a blessing on those who serve"*.

We all turn to the right and move three times widdershins round the room. When the Priestess of Midnight reaches the door it is opened for her by the doorkeeper. Everyone files out and goes upstairs to change their clothes and to keep quiet. They have things to think about and the priestess has things to do.

She places the cauldrons on the hearth, removes the cup and plate, washes them and puts them away. All other candles are left burning, but she trims the wicks before leaving the temple.

X   X   X   X   X

By the time this is done, others will have changed out of their robes and should be ready to do the jobs alloted to them. The men replace the furniture and the women prepare the feast.

Everyone begins to sing and stamp, for we have been travelling in the high realms and need to ground ourselves. For this reason the feast should be substantial and the wine flow freely.

Our party games include all the traditional ones; pass the parcel, musical chairs and a slightly risque one with an orange. As the candles begin to gutter and the fire dies down we gather round and tell horrible ghost stories.

Then people go home, hopefully not looking too carefully behind them.

X X X X X X

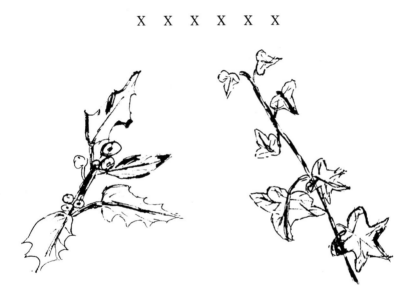

The best incense to use for this rite is the resin of Larches. Go out in a group to where you know some have been cut and simply scoop the resin out of the bark or scrape it from the cut bottom of the tree.

Winter Solstice Trees

The holly is a symbol of life One of the few green trees left in the woods in winter. If chilblains are thrashed with a holly twig they are supposed to go away. Not surprisingly.

There is an old superstition that if you have ivy growing up your walls, you will be protected from witchcraft. I would dearly love to have some. It is about the only keeper-away-of-witches I lack.

The Golden Bough

Mistletoe, the golden bough, is reputed to protect the house from thunder and lightning. I use it to keep my blood pressure down.

Several years ago, just after my eldest son was married, I sent him out in the afternoon of the Solstice to fetch some mistletoe. It was growing very high up on a willow tree which grew aslant a deep river. There had been heavy rain so that the water was about forty feet deep. But Bob was a soldier and had overcome worse hazards. It was growing dusk by the time he actually climbed the willow, which, as I said was high. He picked the bunch, then climbed a little higher to get another. By this time it was quite dark and the wind was getting up. My new daughter-in-law came panting back to the house - Bob was stuck up the tree. My other son had to fire a running line, attached to a cross-bow bolt, over a branch. We hauled up a stout rope, Bob grabbed it but

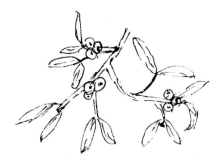

came straight down like a plumb line and dangled over the river. He managed to swing the rope a bit and luckily timed his jump just right and landed on the bank. The moral of this story is, do as Mother says and gather your greenery in daylight or you might not live to tell the tale.

Solstice Symbols

The winter solstice falls right at the end of the sign of Sagittarius, the Archer. This sign rules the Ninth House of the Zodiac which governs philosophy, religion, higher knowledge and travel. Sagittarius is ruled by Jupiter the Bringer of Jollity and planet of expansion. His colour is usually pale blue and his number is 4.

On or around the 21st December the sun passes into the sign of Capricorn, the fish tailed Goat whose symbol was the Horn of Plenty. Dickens caused his Ghost of Christmas Present to carry such a horn, and it is a symbol often used on greetings cards at this time.

The candle was associated with the Roman Saturnalia, and all over Europe candles have been lit especially upon the night of the solstice. Ops, the wife of Saturn, whose most sacred day was 20th December, is remembered in the giving of gifts. The Romans gave presents at this time as a token of love and respect to both friends and relations and also to government officials, from whom they hoped to gain some boon.

The last sheaf of corn, sometimes made into a corn dolly was given to the cows in the byre, to ensure that they gave good milk. This sheaf must have been particularly big because frumenty was made from it, the first meal taken on the morning of the solstice, or later at Christmas.

The Dolly which was often constructed around an apple, was hung in the farm kitchen until the morning of the Solstice, or in some places the morning of Christmas. On this morning, the apple was given to the nicest woman working on the farm, (what criteria the farmer used is open to conjecture) and as stated above, the Dolly was given to the cows.

Holly was always considered to be a male tree, but as we know only the female bears berries. The male has fairly insignificant flowers in July. There are two well known varieties called Silver Queen, which is male and Golden King, which is female. So if you want berries on your holly, go for the King. Most of the native, un-got-at trees which live in what is left of our hedgerows seem to be male these days. The females have all been grubbed out. It might be a useful exercise for an occult group to go round planting female hollies, to bring back colour into our hedgerows in winter.

Everyone knows that the Christmas tree was introduced into the country by the sainted Albert, consort of Victoria. Well, this ain't quite the case. The very earliest Celts to invade the Island brought with them a tradition of planting fir trees and watching the stars through their branches on dark, winter nights. This presumably is where the custom of putting lights on the tree came from. The Celts possibly picked the custom up on their long journey across Europe in the last thousand years before this era.

Then there are the Guizers and Mummers, the Morris Dancers and all the Fire traditions from all over the country. Not all of them firmly attached to the Solstice but so many performed around this time of year that they are closely connected.

> "A room, a room, a garland room
> I come to clear the way
> And many follow after me
> To show you sport and play."

They are mostly performed upon the 26th December, St. Stephen's Day, the first Christian martyr. What this actually has to do with Mumming plays, I'm not sure. The poor tenant workers of the parish had very few days off during the year, they had to squeeze quite a lot of fun into a short time before Plough Monday when they all went back to work.

SAGITTARIUS

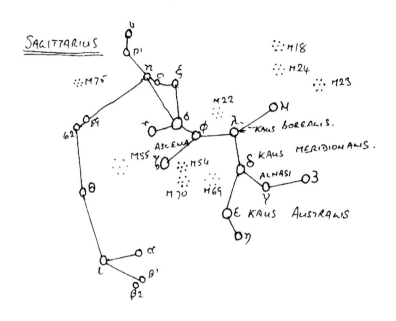

∴ M18

∴ M24

∴ M23

∴ M75

M22
∴

υ
ρ'
η ο ξ
δ φ λ
χ
τ M
KAUS BOREALIS.

KAUS MERIDIONALIS.

62 59

ASCELLA
M55
μ
∴ M54

M70 M69

δ
ALNASI
γ
3

θ

ε KAUS AUSTRALIS

η

α
ι
β'
β2

CAPRICORN.

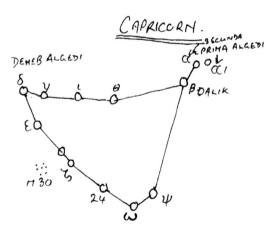

SECUNDA
PRIMA ALGEDI
α² α₁
DENEB ALGEDI
β DABIK

δ ν ι θ

ε

M 30
ρ

24 ω ψ

Halcyon Days

A lovely legend of the Solstice is that of the Halcyon days. These fall seven days before and seven after, the solstice. They were named after Halcyone, wife of Ceyx of Trachis who was drowned at this time of year. Halcyon was so heartbroken that she threw herself into the sea rather than live without her husband. Touched by her devotion, the Gods turned husband and wife into kingfishers. In those days kingfishers were believed to nest on platforms of weeds which floated on calm seas. The Gods promised that whenever kingfishers were brooding, the seas would remain calm.

During this time, one year, I was walking with my dog through the water meadows of the Kennet, near West Kennet Barrow. On a bank a kingfisher sat watching me, I followed it for quite a distance. Each time I caught up it flew further. It led me to a magical place I'd never been before, a still pool with a swan paddling quietly in the middle. It was cold and the snow was deep, but I felt a wonderful sense of warmth all round me.

A Spell ꜰoꜱ Healing

Pick some rue on the night of
the full moon, with your left
hand. As you pick it say:-

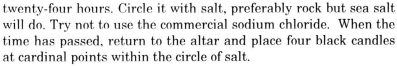

*"Rue, Rue, Pure and True
Cleansing powers I claim of you;
That (name) may no longer be
Suffering from their malady."*

Leave a libation as an offering
to the plant.

Place the rue in a glass of pure
spring water on the altar for
twenty-four hours. Circle it with salt, preferably rock but sea salt
will do. Try not to use the commercial sodium chloride. When the
time has passed, return to the altar and place four black candles
at cardinal points within the circle of salt.

Remember that you have to do this or you will be trying to move
the circle which ain't good.

Light the North candle (Earth) first, saying :- *"This candle is
symbolic of the manifestation of Earth in the disease of (name). By
the power of the Light we abjure it's ability to harm (name)."*

Light the southern candle (Fire) and say:- *"This candle is symbolic
of pain caused to (name) and by the power of the Light, we dissolve
it's ability to cause pain."*

Light the eastern candle (Air) and say:- *"This candle is symbolic of
the mental torment brought to (name). By the power of the Light
we dissolve it's ability to affect (name) mentally."*

Light the western candle (Water) and say:- *"This candle is
symbolic of the barrier to compassion withheld from (name). In the
power of the Light we break down this barrier. This is done in the
names of the Lord and the Lady."*

Leave the candles to burn out, making sure they are safe, naturally. Collect the salt and rue and place them in a small red flannel pouch. Present the pouch to the person for whom the rite has been done as a talisman to aid his or her recovery from the illness. This spell is best done in the latter half of the third quarter of the waning moon.

I must give thanks to Robert Arditti for this spell.

A Blessing Spell for Winter Solstice

We ask a blessing on this house,
This happy Eve of solstice time.
We sing and dance and make carouse
To celebrate deep winter's clime.

For Herne is here, and mistletoe
The Holly and its berries bloom.
We dance a carol, round we go
The Ivy winds about the room.

With wine and cake we make a toast,
And bring a blessing to our host.

Solstice Eve Chant

The geese fly high this Solstice morn,
The woods are bare, the snow is deep.

We wait for Herne to sound His horn
To wake His children up from sleep.

To celebrate this happy night
When winter may be put to flight.

Winter Solstice Chant

Geese and standing stones and mist,
Baying hounds and hooting owl.

Sparkling stars and snow that's crisp
HERNE IS HERE. BRING FORTH THE BOWL

Winter in the Village

The feast of Midwinter comes after the Solstice, and this is when the couple were told to watch for the sunrise, which would tell them that the Sun had begun his journey back from the south. I mentioned the fact that the poor villagers would have been at play from the solstice until Plough Monday, but more of that later.

The whole of Yule was a time of relaxation, for it was not just a couple of days but nearly a month in length, ending on or about the 5th January. Now these dates are modern ones. In the middle of the eighteenth century, Britain changed over from the Julian calender to the Gregorian (or vice versa) and eleven days were lost.

To say that this caused problems was to put it mildly. There were riots and general mayhem all over the island. People were convinced that they had lost several days out of their short lives and were not happy. They had, of course, and that made it worse. Aldermen, beadles, Members of Parliament were besieged by irate tax payers and the poor who didn't pay them. The English, contrary to popular belief, have always delighted in the possibility of a riot. We are not a God-fearing, law abiding lot, and a good riot breaks up the monotony.

The decent burghers wondered if their taxes would be reduced in accord with the loss of days, but the poor were justifiably incensed. Journeymen and 'prentice boys raced through the streets yelling "Give us back our eleven days" and the contemporary equivalent of "You"ve shortened our lives, you******". Various buildings were set on fire and eventually the Riot Act had to be read. I'm not sure that it did a great deal of good, the whole population was really annoyed by this time.

I am a great lover and quoter of Kipling and there are two little bits from his poem "*Norman and Saxon*".

"*The Saxon is not like us Normans,*
His manners are not so polite.
But he never means anything serious till he talks about justice and
  right.
When he stands like an ox in the furrow,
With his sullen eyes set on your own
and grumbles "These ain't fair dealing" my son, leave the Saxon
  alone."

The second, also relevant in this instance, is:-

"*They'll drink every hour of the daylight and poach every hour of*
  the dark.
It's the sport not the rabbits they're after
and we've plenty of game in the park.
Don't hang 'em or cut off their fingers. That's wasteful as well as
  unkind,
For a hard-bitten South-country poacher
makes the best man-at-arms you can find."

There is a lot in that. It is a pity that with the last example I shall give, our lords and masters forgot this advice.

"*Appear with your wife and the children*
at their weddings and funerals and funerals and feasts.
Be polite but not friendly to bishops: be good to all poor parish
  priests.
Say "we" "us" and "ours" when you're talking,
Instead of "you fellows and I",
Don't ride over seeds, keep your temper; **and never you tell 'em a**
  lie."

Now you may think that this is all irrelevant to what I have just written, but read it well. It was and is probably the best advice given to rulers and so many of them forget it, or have never been told. Poachers were tortured and later on, they were deported. Our modern masters forget that they are supposed to be the servants of the people and talk down to us even now and most of all they lie to us.

But, in the fourteenth century they still remembered what happened when the peasants revolted. The men who marched were carrying the greatest weapon in warfare at that time. By the eighteenth century bowmen and archers were no longer important, but there were many wars and the poor were still recruited to serve in the line. So, when they rioted, their masters listened. They did not change back the calender, but they did make real efforts to calm people down.

The whole reason for giving all this information is to throw a light on the calendar as we use it today. Samhaine was on the 11th of November, not October 31st.

The Solstice would have been on 1st of January and Midwinter, or Christmas would have been on the 5th of January and Twelfth Night on the 17th January.

This makes far more sense of all the celebrations. The mumming plays, on or about Boxing Day, the Hunting of the Wren at the New Year and all the Fire games played throughout the land made far more sense in the old calender than in the new. We were far behind Europe, they had changed over to the new calender in the sixteenth century, which is why there are some fairly strange discrepancies as to dates.

There were still all over the country, people who refused to accept the change, and who celebrated Christmas on the above date. Francis Kilvert, for instance, whose 19th century diary was filmed several years ago, insisted that the Thorn at Glastonbury only flowered on the old date. He rode to Radnorshire and was given a sprig "for luck" by his hostess, which must be "put in clear water".

Here endeth the history lesson, for now.

We are talking here about the feast of midwinter, known to most people as Christmas. Witches should not neglect this time. For the very good reason that enormous amounts of good-will abound. It is party time and witches always enjoy a good party. It is a time for giving presents and for overeating and probably overdrinking.

Never run away with the idea that Christmas has become too commercialised. It always was. People ALWAYS ate and drank too much and gave presents they could not afford to people they hardly knew and who didn't want them anyway. It is how the Midwinter rite is observed, very probably from the time of our earliest ancestors. The time of the observable movement of the sun back from the South made people happy and they would have wished to share this good fortune with others. They would have spent the dark time, in the light of the fire in their caves, weaving a special mat, choosing a really good skin or fur or even a splendid joint of venison. Made a basket or a pot or found some pretty shells to make a necklace. All to be given away as a sign of thanks that the year had turned. This was the reason and the object of giving presents.

Which brings me neatly, to one of my special hobby horses. There are so many magazines and occult shops which will sell you anything and everything you need to become a witch. Don't believe it. Witchcraft is a craft. This means making things yourself. Yes, it is great to have a lovely silver cup, after a lifetime in the business, I finally have one myself. But you should make as much of your kit as you can. Only your special touch can make what you use your own.

Jimmy Edwards, a comedian of whom most of you will not have heard, had a catch phrase *"Learn a trade, my son. Learn a trade."* Witchcraft is based upon commonsense not some airy fairy nonsense based on someone's ideas. It is really not cerebral, leave that to cabbalists who do it well and magicians who often try to. Learn how to make corn dollies, your own robes if you wear them, cook things, make the wine for your rites and your own oat cakes Why buy them in a packet from a supermarket when it is far better to bake them yourself. So, they are as hard as bricks, that is good for your teeth and your jaw. It makes you chew. Grow your own herbs. Collect larch resin, plum resin and small apple twigs to make incense. Remember, you will only get resin from trees that have stoned fruit. There is no use at all looking for resin from an apple tree, it is the wood itself that smells so wonderful.

Remember too, that however great a priestess, or priest, you may be, we don't have High Priestesses in the real old religion, you are the Priestess of your own Hearth and NO-ONE has a soul above housework. You may not like it, I don't myself, but the Goddess in Her wisdom has given you your home and you need to honour Her in the way you keep it.

Twelfth Night

This night used to be celebrated with public fires, lit on beacons and headlands, as a way to increase the fertility of the land and its domestic animals. In some counties these fires were dedicated to the prevention of disease and decay in corn crops, by which I mean wheat, barley, oats and to some extent rye.

Farmers would circle a field of twelve fires with a thirteenth in the middle. They would dance round these fires, shouting and beating the ground with ash plants. The first sight of one fire was the cue for the next farm to light theirs. In a short time there would be fires all over the country, and I do mean a short time.

The last time the Beacon fires were lit was for the Queen's 25th. Anniversary the first fire lit on Parliament Hill, and it took only a matter of minutes for the whole string, from the Scillies to the Shetlands to be lit. I was on a hill in Wiltshire where there was great excitement, all of us looking for the first flicker of our own cue. No one who has not witnessed this can realise just how effective the Beacon String is.

This is also the day when the apple orchards are wassailed in Somerset. The whole farming family and all the workers gathered in the orchard to sing to the trees:-

"Here's to thee, ole apple tree,
When thou mayest bud, when thou mayest blow,
And when thou barest apples enow.
Hats full, caps full, big bushel sacks full
And my pockets all full too.
Hooray, Hooray, Hoo Ya."

Hip, Hip Hooray, was one of the most ancient calls to the Oak, as Lord of the Forest. As was Hey, Nonny Nonny. In some places the trees were sprinkled with cider and cider soaked bread was pushed into the axillary branches. My grandfather never bothered with cider, he used his own urine, straight from the source. We had splendid apples.

Branches of Juniper were burned and the ashes sprinkled in the cattle stalls, as a protection against the evil eye for the coming year. Very few junipers grow wild now, the last I saw were on Brean Down, on the Bristol Channel, but I rather expect most of those have been destroyed to make way for the bridge.

All the greenery should have been taken outside and burned on the very last day of the Solstice fires. It is said to be very unlucky to find even one stray leaf hiding behind a cushion or under the sofa. You need to say a little spell for each one you find and take it outside carefully, saying:-

"*I did not mean to leave thee*
Thy friends have long been gone,
To burn alone will grieve thee
So go back to thine own."

You should then place the leaf under the tree from which you took
it.

Plough Monday

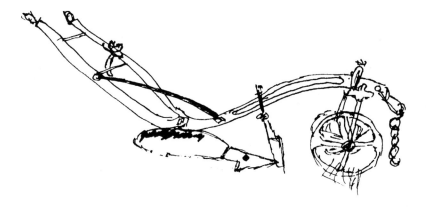

The first Monday after Twelfth Night and the end of all
festivities, so decreed King Alfred, and it was back to work. The
ritual of blessing the plough took place where four fields met, or
four farms, four parishes or even four counties. You can still see
some of the great marker stones, they have not yet all been
uprooted.

The Mummers were out in force and as it was the last day most
farm workers would have off for a year, they made the most of it.
They danced round a decorated plough, leaping high to show the
wheat how to grow. The plough was drawn through the village,
followed by a man dressed in animal skins and green twigs, leaves
being hard to come by at this time of the year.

This Green Man capered with a begging bowl. It was a way of supplementing a very poor income and would today be termed as "demanding money with menaces."

The middle class maintained that all the money collected was spent in the inn the same night, but the poor were not quite so indigent and it was usually shared out between the most needy families. The ubiquitous Corn Dolly, if it had not been given to the cattle, or the most comely woman on the farm, or burned as an offering, was buried in the first furrow cut the following day. She was a well travelled lass, this Corn Dolly.

The church took over this festival, as it took over most of the others and in many churches the dressed plough is blessed, in the nave, this was in the days of the hand plough, which could be man-handled through the doors leaving the great shire horse which pulled it standing at the vestry door.

Now, it is more likely to be a giant Massey-Ferguson or an old Fordson tractor, standing outside the Lych Gate. Few of the old dances accompany this blessing.

Hedges cut in January should be cut from East to West, which is fine, if your hedge runs that way. There is always a snag. A friend of mine insists that herbs should be picked from the North side of the hedge, early in the morning, BEFORE the dew falls, (how early can you get?). You can only do this, of course, if the hedge does run East-West. If it runs North-South, or even at an angle you are stuck, stymied and even up the creek. Oh. Yes. You must pick them with your left hand and with no iron.

Either you have to have extremely strong and sharp nails or you have mastered the art of flint-knapping. Some herbs wouldn't be seen dead on the north side of a hedge, anyway.

No, these old saws had a reason, but I'm afraid that few of them are even mildly useful now. Why pick herbs BEFORE the dew is on them? Nights, even in the height of summer are often damp and damp herbs get mouldy very quickly. I pick mine when the dew is off 'em, later in the morning. I use a sharp knife or scissors, because I no longer wear a short tunic made from skins and I am not afraid of metal, whichever one it is. I even chop them in my Magimix or in a very useful hachette, with a curved bladed knife. It is best to use what is to hand. Some more Kipling, from a poem called "*The King's Job*".

"The wisest thing, we suppose, that a man can do for his land
Is the work that lies under his nose, with the tools that lie under
  his hand."

Chapter Three

IMBOLC

You shall on Candlemas Day
throw candle and candlestick away.

The Goddess returns from the Otherworld and the Earth rejoices. Before the advent of the calender, be it Gregorian or Julian, we used nature's own to show us when this auspicious event would be. Spring arrives with the thaw and the first Snowdrops. I have heard it said that the Snowdrop is not a native of this country and was introduced by monks in the fifteenth century. The name, they say, comes from the German "*schneeglockchen*' which means "snowbell'. The reason for this idea is that Shakespeare makes no mention of it. But so far as I know, he doesn't mention dandelions either, but that does not mean they weren't here.

> *"Lone Flower, hemmed in with snows and white as they*
> *but hardier far, Once more I see thee bend thy forehead*
> *As if fearful to offend, like an unbidden guest*
>
> *Yet thou art welcome as a friend whose zeal outruns*
> *His promise. Nor will I then thy modest grace forget*
> *Venturous harbinger of the Spring."*
>
> Wordsworth

The old names for the snowdrop were 'blackbird flower', Candlemas Bells, Fair-Maids-of-February, Snow Piercer and several others. It was also called Death's Flower. February was a notorious month for death, especially that of small children.

So, Spring arrives with the thaw and the snowdrops and with it comes the Goddess. Urban dwellers seldom notice the change of seasons. If they walk to work they might notice that the

Municipal Parks employers have dug the ground over, prior to the well-regimented displays of later in the year. But how many will notice that beneath the trees the snowdrops have put in an appearance.

I should have headed this chapter with a song from *"On a Clear Day"*, which starts:

"Hey buds below, up is where to grow
Up with which below can't compare with
Hurry, it's lovely up here."

A nice song to sing to the Earth on
this morning.

In our strange climate the thaw
might not come until March and
we have even had snow in June but our festivals began when the climate was more stable. The Goddess comes and we can if we stop and listen, hear and smell the change in the air. There may not be a green leaf to be seen, but the snowdrops never fail, the Snow Piercer fears neither ice nor heavy frost.

The Precession of the Seasons has proceeded according to precedent and all is well. In olden times, farmers used to remove their trousers and sit upon the cold ground to feel if the ground was now warm enough to plough.

In the Christian Calender this day is known as Candlemas and is the Purification of the Blessed Virgin Mary. Why should a virgin need to be purified? For many thousands of years, 40 days after the Winter Solstice there was a festival sacred to women.

The Festival of Imbolc (literally the time of the Ewe's Milk) and the Return of the Goddess were celebrated only by the women of the tribe. I am not sure what the men did. Perhaps this was the beginning of the All-Male Club. It would be amusing to think that the illustrious Athenium began as a retreat for indigent men when the women were otherwise engaged.

The festival would have been celebrated upon the Eve, that is the evening before the day. This is the old way of doing things, but this rite is about the end of Winter and the quiet joy we feel that the dark, cold time is nearly over. If we do this properly we should then rest before the second half of the rite, done early in the morning of the next day.

This should be a more restrained rejoicing, quieter than other festivals. We are, after all, welcoming the Maiden, who bears within her the Spring, conceived last Beltaine Eve, April 30th. We should feel the re-awakening of the Earth. It is about Birth and new beginnings. Doing rites in two parts like this means that you can reinforce the idea with yourselves that the Witches Year ends and begins at every season and that both should be recognised.

The flowers used at Imbolc should all be white and the candles the same. If you can find enough snowdrops you can make little chaplets to encircle the base of the candles and perhaps a few to entwine with ivy to make chaplets for your heads. But NEVER a bunch of snowdrops for this purpose, that would be unlucky. The Snowdrop, as well as being a symbol of purity is also called the Death Flower, because, as I remarked above, February was a month that filled the churchyard.

Looking back over what I have written, it might be confusing to think of a Maiden who is pregnant. I can only say that she is like a heifer, who is a heifer until she has dropped her first calf.

In olden times, because we were a Nature and not a Solar religion, we did not feel that the Sun was growing stronger. It doesn't. The days may be longer but February is usually the coldest month, in fact the coldest day of the year was reckoned to be the 13th. So we gave thanks for the increase in light, we are a pragmatic bunch and like to keep the odds in our favour.

We also give thanks for the new life that is all around us. The birds are getting busy, and noisy, and will soon be nesting, if some idiot doesn't decide to cut the hedges they might begin to rebuild last year's site or look round for a new one. If you have nesting boxes, do make sure they have been repaired well before this time. Old nesting materials can hold disease and if you treat them with a wood preserver late, the birds won't use them; they dislike the smell of chemicals.

Who ever said that flocks were peaceful. To the urban dweller coming into the countryside for a refresher, they might look lovely skipping about and lying quietly but if you live in the countryside you will know from experience that these periods of peace are short-lived to say the least. No-one who has lived on the other side of a fence from five hundred or so ewes calling for one thousand lambs would agree. Sheep do not all sound the same, there is

hell's own choir out there with sopranos, tenors, contraltos and even a few basses and the one thousand lambs, bless their little fluffy hearts all yell and scream for their mums at the same time.

On top of this you have the birds who are not, as some people suppose, calling out their joy of living and the delights of the day to come but are threatening to beat the living daylights out of any other bird that invades their territory.

If you have ever had the misfortune to have a starling build a nest, or rather lay it's eggs in your attic you will not be pleased at the screeching noise which wakens you at the first glimpse of light. It is not a pleasant noise, the one made by the young of the species. Starting up from a deep sleep you might think that something is being strangled. Then you realise what the noise is and you lie there gloomily thinking about the mess they will make of your loft insulation when they start gallumphing about.. Which they do. Birds do not tippy toe. They gallumph and what is more they do it in army boots.

The Rite

We have, on occasions, turned this into a Rite of Blessing for the Land. Stating our objects, which are usually threefold:

1. Greeting the aspect of the Goddess then appearing in the sky; timed right this should be just before the first quarter after the snow thaws.

2. Telling the Maiden of the Earth's need for Her return.

3. Thanking the Holly Lord, Herne, for His protection.

We go one to ask the Mother aspect, the Full, that as She begins to wane She takes with Her the bad weather, the floods and rain, so that the land may dry out and the crops may grow.

As the Moon governs the tides and nearly all aspects of water, and as the Waning Moon is the time for what are often called 'banishments' or getting rid of untoward influences this is as good a time as any to do this.

As we greet the Maiden thus:-

> *"On this night we remember the Goddess who left us as Crone at Samhaine and is to return to us.........*
> *Come back to us Lady and bring the Spring."*

> *"Lady, the snowdrops have pushed their way through the cold, wet earth and we dream of Your return.*
> *Come back to us, Lady, and bring the Spring."*

> *"The plants which went down with you are close to renewal.*
> *Come back to us, Lady, and bring the Spring."*

> *"Come from the Caves of Annwn, where souls are purged of pain and sorrow.*
> *Return from Hel, where souls are purged of grief and despair.*
> *Come to us from the Mists of Avalon, from the Isle of Apples.*
> *Come from Tir-nan-Og, land of Blessed Rest.*
> *Return from the Land of Faerie, where you have dreamed long of summer."*

> *"Come back to us, Lady, and bring the Spring."*

This rite is done by five people, each standing at a point of a pentagram. Each one says a line and then all say the *"Come back to us, Lady...."* This gives a good balance. Between each part of the rite we hand round mead and oatcakes.

The colours of the Goddess are:- White for the Maiden, Red for the Mother and Black for the Crone. These are the colours worn by three women who perform another rite, which can be used for a larger group. These extra people stand in a circle and watch and dance at the given time.

As the three dance, they chant:-

"Come to us from the Earth's four quarters
Earth and Air, and Fire and Water,
Bring your minions to this home
Sylphs, Undines, Salamanders, Gnomes,
Ask your Captains, Nixsa, Djinn, Paralda, Ghob
To bring them in."

I cannot quote this rite at length because I did not write it. It was written by Patricia Harril-Morris who kindly gave me permission to quote these few lines. As you almost assuredly know, each of the Quarters has an Elemental and it is ruled by a King. Ghob is the King of the Gnomes of Earth; Paralda, King of Air and Sylphs; Nixsa, King of the Water Undines and Djinn, King of the Salamanders of Fire.

This can be quite long and very energetic, involving a lot of dancing. If you are not fit you are liable to get breathless and get the words disastrously mixed up, as I did, gasping words which I hoped no one understood. The Kings' names came out as something like Alexander's Silk Undies.

This is NOT a rite for old ladies to undertake. If you are unfit and ancient, stick to the sidelines and watch.

Many people move house in the Spring and some like to have a blessing for their new home. An old one and one I often use is:-

"Who comes to me, I keep.

Who goes from me, I free.

Yet against all I stand

Who do not carry my key."

As an inscription over a door, with three pinecones hanging down to blow in the wind, this is hard to beat as a blessing, but if you feel in need of more;-

84

Hang an ash bough over the door.
Fill your pockets with iron nails
Carry always a leaf of mullein.

But say these words against the worst..........

"I stand.......In circles of Light......That nothing...May cross."

There was a law, legislated by Alfred the Great, that no candle should be lit after Candlemas. Which is why the Saxons held a festival of lights to use all the bits up.

Before you throw your candle away or burn it, as instructed by He who was called Great, I think he won a battle or six, especially one really special one at sea against the Vikings. It, the candle, can tell you many things. If sparks came from the wick, strangers would come to your door.

If you light a candle from a fire, you can expect to die in poverty.

And I am told that a candle left to burn out brings really bad luck. Which is a pity, because whenever we do a rite, the special candles are ALWAYS left to do just that. Perhaps it is different if they are left "a'purpose"

Ashgrove Esbat

Another name for this time is the Ashgrove Esbat. The Ash is one of the three magical trees, with Oak and Thorn. It was Yggdrassil, the tree upon which Odin hung for nine days and nights, before he lost an eye and was given in return knowledge of the Runes, after which he was reborn.

It is the World Tree, and ancestor of the Man Kind. A dangerous tree to destroy or to cut down, but an Ash plant is the most useful quarter staff and of course, the arrows of many battles were made from straight branches a "clothyard long." It is thought to protect one from lightning.

Often associated with Merlin as the Archmage, because it is a tree of intelligence and initiation, and it can be used for divination and charms. Do remember that a stick is for pointing with. Unless it is an arrow.

86

It is supposed to protect one from witchcraft. I have them growing all round my house. Perhaps it thinks I need protection because each time I go out into the garden, there is another sport. I wonder if they are trying to tell me something?

A child who had suffered a rupture or who had rickets was passed through a split sapling and this was supposed to cure them. My grandfather had several which were used for this purpose. They must never be cut down or the disease or rupture would return.

The name comes from the Anglo-Saxon "aesc" which was a name used in poetry for spear.

It is nearly always the last tree to come into leaf, despite the old saying:-

"Oak before the Ash and we'll only have a splash.
Ash before the Oak and we're bound to have a soak."

It is hardly ever in leaf before May and is usually the first to lose its leaves in autumn. One of the reasons given for this tardiness is that witches were supposed to eat the buds on their way to the Beltaine rites, so to spite them the tree don't grow the buds until Midsummer, when they will be well looked after by St. John.

Imbolc Birds

The peacock, believed by many people to be very unlucky, is traditionally associated with this time. It was thought to be unlucky to bring in the tail feathers because of the eye which seemed to stare out at one.

In England, the bird's unearthly cry is thought to be the voice of the Devil calling to the soul of the newly dead, but it also foretells bad weather, especially thunder and lightning. In India, however, it warns of tigers in the vicinity.

The proud sun-loving Peacocke with his feathers
Walkes all along, thinking himself a king.
And with his voice prognosticates all weathers
Although,God knows, how badly he doth sing.

Chester (*Loves Martyr*)

I would rather put the marsh tit in place of the peacock. Whenever we have a cold February, this little bird visits my bird table. I also love to watch the rooks at this time. They fly amazing patterns but it doesn't matter how many birds form the tumbling flocks  or how intricate the patterns are, they always sort themselves into pairs. They fly apart to do their aerobatics, but each returns to its mate between stunts. The old superstition that if rooks build high they foretell a good summer is nonsense. In the wettest of summers, rooks have built exceptionally high. In fact, most of them merely repair the nests of previous years.

Some of the old sayings are:

"When rooks seem to drop in their flight, it foreshadows heavy rain." "The 'tumbling' of rooks is a sure sign of rain."

"When rooks fly high in air, it shows windy storms are very near." This also applies if they congregate on dead branches; stay home all day; feed in the streets or fly to the mountains. In fact, every saw concerning rooks speaks of bad weather to come.

"And see yon rooks, how odd their flight
They imitate the gliding kite.
And seem precipitate to fall
As if they felt the piercing ball.
"Twill surely rain - I see with sorrow
Our jaunt must be put off tomorrow."

Dr. Erasmus Darwin (1731-1802)

Imbolc Symbols

Astrologically, Imbolc falls under the dominion of both Saturn and Uranus - both rulers of the sign of Aquarius. It governs social matters, friendships, group relationships and certain aspects of magic. Saturn is the planet of barriers, self-discipline and hard work, while Uranus is the planet of dramatic change, invention and freedom. I find the idea of both freedom and barriers, difficult to equate, but certainly hard work goes with invention which must always be bound by barriers or from splitting the atom inventors can make nasty bombs, and many inventions have gone haywire without self-discipline. Too much freedom in invention can be chaotic.

It seems such a pity that this gigantic planet, 75,000 miles in diameter yet the weight of any planet in the Solar system, should be associated with the heaviest of Earth metals, and should be thought of as old age and stiffness.

It is a planet of ethereal beauty, but has a highly poisonous atmosphere.

Uranus, on the other hand, is smallish, 32,375 miles in diameter, green and has an atmosphere that is icy and composed of methane, helium, hydrogen and ammonia. There is a possibility of water.

The colour, according to astrology, is amethyst or violet and as one of the spring flowers is the violet this is quite to be expected, as is the gemstone. This is Amethyst, (although one of my books quotes Chalcedony.

The Tarot card is the Star, which symbolises Hope, perhaps that the freedom of all these inventions does not blow us all to Kingdom come. It also stands for bright prospects for the future. Perhaps that is a hope that all that hard work and invention will bring peace and goodwill. And that is a hope.

I should confess here that I know very little about either Astrology or Crystals. I do however, know quite a bit about Astronomy and rocks. I do have to rely on friends' knowledge and books for these subjects and they can be rather at variance with one another, so, if I say that something is one thing and you think it is another, look at another book.

An Imbolc Spell

Cold winter has gone, the snow will thaw,
The badger stirs within the Earth.
We sing the Goddess back once more
To give the land its own re-birth.

The snowdrop comes, the robin sings
Come now the Maiden
And with one voice
In spring and Love and Goddess we rejoice.

An Imbolc Carol

We dance the Ring of Imbolc
We dance the round of Spring
We dance tonight to invoke
The hope that it will bring.

Casting a Circle

This can be used when casting a circle. It was written by a friend.

'Hearken to the words of Power, used at the appointed hour. Time and Space apart shall be, Things of Wonder we shall see.
Circle pure, most clear and bright, Conjured here by all our might.'

Chapter Four

The Vernal Equinox

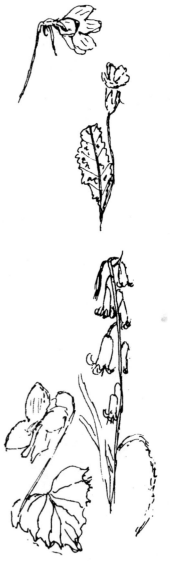

The Earth is quickening. The Birch, Hawthorn and Elder are showing their first leaf buds. The leaves of wood dog roses are already green. Violets, primroses, wood anemones and bluebells are showing above the earth, some in full flower, others waiting their time. Down by the brook the celandines are beginning to cover the snowdrops and the earth has the lovely smell of growing things.

Probably, and I say this advisedly, the snow will have gone but it is still a case of keeping fingers crossed and one day we look out of the window and see the first greening of the corn fields. The blackthorn, which always blossoms before it grows leaves is foaming white, but this is a warning, there is such a thing as a blackthorn winter, when the snow and cold weather come back again.

The lambs are skipping out in the meadow and close to me there are both foxes' earths and badger setts, so early in the morning or just as it gets dusk the young cubs might be seen playing. I spent a long time, one year, standing quietly on a hill watching a fox watching the lambs. My dog was still, not quite sure what I was looking at, then a hare broke from the bank and she gave chase. The fox looked in my direction and saw that there was no danger from the dog, but I raised my walking stick and he obviously thought it was a gun. He was off like a streak of red lightning.

I have the sky charts issued by the Royal Astronomical Society for the past six years and I am here to tell you that in that time most of the Vernal Equinoxes have been on the 20th March and, with two exceptions, early in the morning. This information is from charts drawn up for the Latitude of London which is 51.30 North, as you are no doubt aware, about 0.01 West Longitude. This is the time when the Sun crosses the Celestial Equator and the sun goes into Aries, I am not going to give you all the astronomical data, because you probably know it better than me.

Remember, any work you do in magic is done more easily if you work with the tides, not just of the sea, but of the Moon and the Earth herself. I rarely work on a full moon, for instance, except to go out and tell her how lovely she is. Thank you Ma'am for showing your beauty to the earthbound.

This is not laziness, for I do it every month BUT, think for a moment. At the time of the High Tide, the sea is where it wants to be. It has finished the journey. It won't come any further and at that point it is neither coming, nor going. It is the same with the Moon. Work as much as you like for growth, while She is growing but to me, it is a waste of time to try to work while she is standing still.

No one puts out to sea until the tide begins to move again, so after a day or so, you can begin to work. Not negative magic, that is not necessary, but the ebb tide takes things away and that is what is meant by 'banishments'. Now you are working with the tide itself. As it goes out it can take with it all sorts of rubbish. Put your little cares and worries in a bottle and watch them float away. Do this with the Moon, using a symbolic bottle and you will be surprised how this little bit of magic works wonders for you. Do make sure that you put a self-destruct spell upon it, or they might wither float back or someone else may let the genie out and you will be passing on your problems to someone else. Which ain't good magic, folks.

A word about "banishment". This is always made to look "black", "evil" and very negative in a lot of books on witchcraft. This is another of those nonsenses I"m trying to clear up. YOU are not going to banish anyone, anywhere and you might as well understand this. If you try, you'll come badly unstuck. Three times three is a good thing to remember because that is how you will get it. Straight between the eyes.

Think of it this way. If you are asked to do a healing for anyone, do you begin in the middle? Do you start to heal before you have cleaned the wound? Would you work on anyone's luck BEFORE you have cleared away the dross? My favourite analogy for this is redecorating a room. If you are wise, you will wash down the walls, or if they are papered, clean the old paper off and THEN wash the walls. Few people would be silly enough to paint or paper over grubby surfaces. So you begin by cleaning away.

A second instance is in the garden. You need to clear away the weeds before you plant something new and if your garden has as much bindweed and couch grass as mine, you need to dig deep.

A surgeon cuts away a growth before expecting a healing. So use this time of the month to cut out, dig out, clean out everything you need to get rid of. Do begin with yourself. Get rid of the bugs first.

The best time to do this is about three days after the last quarter, the Crone is very good at taking this sort of stuff with her and the tide is still running fast. When the Moon returns you can begin work for growth, good luck, good health, a bugless atmosphere, a brickless garden or even, if you must, a new love.

Banishings are not very well liked when worded "May he get lost" but are better received as "May he be happy in some other place, with someone else." This is a doctrine of perfection and possibly just a little pious but THEY prefer it and will be more prepared to help.

So it is with the Equinox. Work with the tide of the year. See what you have learned. Put what you really do not need into the little bottle. Say goodbye and be ready for the next phase. The growing of Light.

The fight between the Light and the Dark is not the same as that between the Oak and the Holly. Do not mix or combine them. For one thing, the equinoxes were not really important to the Old Ones. There are very few rituals in hereditary or family magic which even mention it. Naturally, they knew when the days became equal and then longer,(or shorter) but they did not celebrate it. It has, however, become important to modern thinking, so get it right.

We are talking her about the Growth of Light, not the seasonal punch up between the Oak and the Holly. Look in the woods. The Oak has not even begun to put out its green and is probably still wearing last year's brown leaves. These will not go until the new buds push them off the twigs and although the Blackthorn may be in blossom, the Hawthorn certainly is not.

You cannot have a confrontation if only one participant is present. So this rite is for the turning of the year and the MIDDLE of Spring and is not about the winning of the hand, and all that goes with it, of the Maiden. This happens at Beltaine.

The rite really must be done out of doors, preferably in a meadow, possibly with those noisy lambs close by. I do not advise you to do this in the middle of a field of new green corn. You will not make a good friend of the farmer if you do.

Also, do not have dogs near lambs. My farmer used to join us to bless the fields and crops, this might now be against some regulation or other. Heaven forfend that we should get something our neighbours don't have.

It should be done at sunrise, or better still as the season actually turns. If you can arrange to get your folk there just before, you can think of the season which is passing and we can do our own private banishings. Stand in a circle and think of the time when the cold and frost gripped the land. think of all we learned in the season of stillness and give away what we do not need.

This will have had much thought before you come into the circle. You must learn to sift out what you cannot use. Now is the time to begin using the knowledge for this will be not only the time of growing light and fading dark but the beginning of the magical working year when we begin working outside and learning about the land and the magic we hope to use.

It is time to get our feet off the mantle piece, roll up our sleeves and get out into the woods and fields to do some real work.

As the Sun comes up or the time of the Equinox arrives, two men, representing the Dark and the Light, fight each other. It is neither a long nor a hard fight but represents the eternal struggle between the two opposites, which the Light must win if the Man kind of the Earth is to survive. Once the Dark is defeated he retires to the circle, leaving the centre to the Light.

He should not go away completely. Remember that this represents the real world, and however short it becomes, we still have Night. Hopefully, the Sun will win free from the horizon and we raise a shout of "*Hail, god of Light. Welcome to the Lord of the Sun*".

There should be a circle dance and possibly a song about the coming abundance of the Earth. We drink wine, but not too much, many people will be going to work after this but we can eat cake. Then we close and go to breakfast. Do remember to ask a blessing on the work and for the strength to do it.

The Vernal Equinox Tree

Alder
Alnus glutinosa
Fearn

This is the season of the Alder, a tree sacred to Bran, one of the earliest British Gods. His head was supposed to be under the hill of the White Tower, the great citadel of the Tower of London. Britain was thought to be inviolate while it remained there, but there was a rumour that Arthur removed it, saying that he was all the security the island needed.

The ravens which live around the tower were Bran's birds and they too give everlasting security, so long as they remain. Some of their flight feathers are removed to ensure this security. In this world nothing should be left to chance.

The Alder is the fourth tree in the year and the fourth in the Tree Alphabet. It has many folk names, variations on Alder and some interesting ones, like Owl tree, Glase Bush in Devon and Irish Mahogany in Ireland, naturally. It always grows near water and stays green much longer than any other deciduous tree because of the thick, resinous quality of its leaves. The wood is water resistant and so is often used to make the piles of bridges. The Rialto Bridge in Venice is built upon such piles as is Winchester Cathedral which was built on land that was very marshy. There is a statue in the nave of the diver who went down to repair them in the last century.

The houses built on the Somerset levels, known as the Summerlands because that was the only time they were above water, were also built on alder stilts and I believe that the roads made across the marshes were of alder logs.

97

It burns really slowly and makes the best charcoal, particularly for making gunpowder.

It is also the best wood for making clogs, since the wood does not conduct heat well, so keeps the feet warm and cosy. Clog makers would scour the countryside to find a stand, pay good money for the wood, always plant a tree for one cut down, and sell the chippings to dyers. Good Businessmen.

One of the ancient riddles of Bran was

"What can no house ever contain?"

and the answer was

"The piles upon which it is built."

The tree was important to the dying industry, four good dyes can be extracted from it. Red from the bark, green from the flowers, brown from the twigs and pink from the little cones which grow in autumn. These take two years to mature, one year green and the second black. The cones, like those of all cone bearing trees are female. Seeds grow in the green cones and are released the second year when they have turned black.

The small male flowers bloom from about March 18th, the beginning of the fourth month. In due time the pollen is released and fertilises the seed, which falls into the water. It can live in water for over a year and remain fertile. According to Robert Graves, this tree was always considered to be sacred because, when its wood is cut it is white and then turns scarlet as though bleeding. It is a tree of fire, embodying the power of fire over water just as the Sun warms the Earth after the wet, cold days of early Spring.

98

In Ossian's *Song of the Forest*, it is called *"the very battle-witch of all woods, the tree that is hottest in the fight."*

There is a legend that whistles were made from the bark of the alder, by beating the trunk with a willow strip. The bark then became detached and more easily pulled away. This use of willow, was thought to suggest that the whistles were used by witches to conjure up strong winds.

Again, according to Graves, the singing Head of Bran would have been an alder-pipe. At Harlech, where the head sang for seven years there was a mill-stream running past the Castle Rock which was a likely place for an alder grove.

Its day is Saturday, which equates it with Saturn. Bran is also often associated with Saturn. In the Sirens' Welcome to Cronos, they sing:

> *"Through a thick growing alder-wood We clearly see*
> *But are not seen, Hid in a golden haze."*

The Sirens are the Birds of Rhiannon who sang at Harlech in the myth of Bran.

The leaves and green cones make a splendid addition to incense made for the vernal equinox, because, as you will have read above, they are full of resin. Add Myrrh, Rue, (known as the Herb of Grace), Cypress and Vervain. Do use natural ingredients if you can, they are naturally much more personal.

As an addition to Bran-Saturn-Cronos incenses they have no equal and smell much nicer that Asafoetida. Such an incense can be used after funerals and when healing diseases or destroying pests.

Spring Flowers

As Imbolc is a white festival, so this one is green and yellow. Use green and yellow candles, yellow flowers. Everyone should have their own small bunch tied tastefully with a yellow ribbon. Primroses, cowslips (be careful where you pick these, they are protected. I grow my own.) You can put in daffodils but do remember that they are poisonous and will kill anything they are mixed with. This little bunch should be left at the site of the rite as an offering to the Spring Maiden.

Primroses stand for New Love and are supposed to say "*I may learn to love you, it is too soon to tell*". Cowslips speak of sweetness. Daffodils are not encouraging but jonquils hope for an affirmative answer.

Heartsease, the little hardy violet, the tri-colour, is one of the first herbs to show. It is attributed to Venus and therefore to love. The country name is "Love-in-Idleness" and it is used in love potions, spells and chants. There is a fable that it was turned purple by Cupid's bow. Medieval herbalists used it frequently for strengthening the heart.

A love potion of heartsease can be made with half a pint of good red wine. Add two tablespoons of the dried flowers, using fresh ones you need more, and two or three cloves and one tablespoon of clear honey. Allow to infuse for ten minutes, then serve hot.

An old way to tell the future was to pick a wild pansy. It doesn't work if the flower is bought. Count the lines on the petals.

Four	indicate that your wish will come true
Five	that there is trouble coming, but you should overcome it.
Six	a surprise will come to you
Seven	you have a faithful sweetheart
Eight	your sweetheart may be fickle
Nine	you will marry overseas.

If the centre line is longest, you must announce your engagement on Sunday.

Do not pick a wild pansy when it is sprinkled with dew drops, this could mean the death of a loved one.

> *"A violet by a mossy bank, half hidden from the eye*
> *Fair as a star, when only one is shining in the sky."*

That was part of a poem by Wordsworth called *"Lucy"* but the first poem I ever learned, when I was about four is still engraved on my mind.

" I know, blue modest violet, beaming with dew at morn.
I know the place you come from and the way that you were born.
When God cuts holes in Heaven, the holes that stars peep through
The little scraps fall down to Earth. The little scraps are you."

The chief herb of this time must be the violet. Also associated with Venus and with water and according to the old herbals protected one from "wykked spectyres".

If you pick the first one you see in Spring, it will bring you good luck. The ancient Greeks used to wear them to bring peace and sleep.

A chaplet of flowers was a cure for dizziness and headaches and the smell is said to calm the temper. I must remember to wear some. My Granny's favourite seat was covered in them, and she used the scent a lot. Her temper, like my mother's (and mine) was pretty volcanic, so perhaps neither of them, (nor me) wear it often enough.

Here is a Love Spell for the Vernal Equinox.

Violet and lavender, take each a few
Enclose them with Myrtle of dark green hue.
Make them in a posy, small and round and bright
You may see your true love in your dreams tonight.

In the Middle Ages, the bedroom to be used by a bridal couple was fumigated with burning brambles as a magical protection for the couple against the possible ill-wishing by jealous rivals. This is not a delightful smell and was done well in advance of the wedding. It had to be counter-acted by strewing the floor with sweet smelling herbs, like verbena, mint, and above all violet. A water was made from the violets as well and sprinkled round the room, just before the couple entered the room. The pillows would have been stuffed with some of the same mixture, with a preponderance of violets.

What happened if the couple suffered from hay fever I would not like to guess. Perhaps a difficult night was put down to the ill-wishing.

This lovely little flower was thought to bring faithfulness so was included in wedding bouquets. The idea of giving the young couple a tea set, or at least a plate decorated with the flower was thought to keep this idea in mind. It's a thought.

According to Geoffrey Grigson perfume raised the violet from its wild obscurity more than two thousand years ago. The perfume suggested sex and so the flower was dedicated to the all the European goddess of love.

It was also used by the early physicians who made it into Oil of Violets and Syrup of Violets as well as perfume. It was held to be soothing, cool and bland. They gave to gardens their "chiefest beauty and most gallant grace" (Gerard) and "stir up a man to do that which is comely and honest".

The Goodman of Paris, Le Menagier de Paris, who wrote a book on *Moral and Domestic Economy* in 1393 suggests using the flowers in salads and sauces, with eggs and in puddings. This is probably where our own crystallised flowers come from.

The Equinox Bírð

There would seem to be two of these, the Nightingale and the Swallow and for the life of me I cannot decide which would be the most important. so I will try to give you a little idea of both. They actually come together in a Greek myth. Philomena and Procne were sisters. King Tereus of Daulis married Procne with whom he had a son, then he cut out her tongue and hid her away in the country, proclaiming her death in order to marry Philomena. In the usual rather bloody sequence of Greek mythology, (I've always wondered if they were both either very beautiful or very wealthy) Procne gets word to Philomena, she is found and in vengeance kills her son. Tereus goes after them with an axe and the Gods, ever helpful, changed them into birds. Philomena into a nightingale and Procne into a swallow. Tereus was changed into a hoopoe. It is all to do with oracles.

Swallow   *Hirundines rusticae*

The migrants come at the earliest in the latter days of March, not in a grat sweep but in small groups and they stay until Michaelmas day or a little later when they gather together on telegraph wire, stay for a day or so and then they are gone. I always watch them with not a little sorrow, as they gather,

because it means that summer is over and the winter draws nigh. You can never know when they arrive, the old saying "*One swallow does not make a summer*" is so right, but you always know when they leave. In White's "*Natural History of Selbourne*" the reverend gentleman mentions them gathering in a neighbour's walnut tree, "where they had taken up lodgings for the night. At the dawn of the day, which was foggy, they all rose together in infinite numbers, occasioning such a rushing from the strokes of their wings against the hazy air, as might be heard to a consider-able distance."

They can be seen most often flying fast and low over rivers, collecting midges and small flying insects and they wash themselves by dropping into the water as they fly. Their flight is full of tight high G. force turns and they remind me of the Spitfires I watched during the wonderful summer of 1940 when they swooped, climbed and banked after German bombers and fighters.

Swallows build saucer-shaped nests of mud and dried grass lined with feathers and unlike the swift's which are almost circular, these are open at the top. Ringing has proved that the same birds come back to the same nesting places year after year. These used to be mainly in farm buildings, but we have become so obsessed with hygiene nowadays that there are few insects to be seen in milking parlours, although they used to be called 'chimney swallows' and nested about five feet down inside the chimney. These have largely gone too, so the poor creatures are finding it difficult to find a home. They lay between three and six eggs which are white and heavily speckled with red-brown spots.

It sings both on the wing and while perching. They are brave little birds and should a sparrow-hawk appear they gang up on it and chase it, buffeting it with their small bodies until it flies off. They also stike at cats who presume to get too close to the nests. They seem to like flying in a strong wind, which is unusual and if you have ever ridden across a down, they will accompany you for miles, sweeping round the horse and scoffing the insects disturbed by the hooves.

Swallows are easily distinguished from martins and swifts by the shape of their wings and the long forks to their tails. They also have a bright chestnut patch beneath the beak and a pinkish patch just in front of the tail.

There is a lovely little story about a swallow building a nest in the body of an owl, which hung dead from a rafter in a barn. The owl, nest and eggs were sold to a collector who gave the donor a great conch shell to hang in the same place. The female duly laid her second batch of eggs in the shell.

Mythologically, the swallow is a fire bird, one of those who brought fire from heaven. The swallow was bringing the fire which burned a hole in its tail, hence the red spot. The wren caught the fire and succeeded in bringing it to Earth thereby losing its own feathers.

In one legend the Devil throws a flaming brand which caused the red spots, beneath beak and tail and in another it was the swallow who brought fire to Earth after the Deluge, and in the myth of the eagle and the wren it is said that the eagle was so

105

angry at being tricked by the wren that he set the swallow to guard her for ever.

The swallow is also associated with water because yet another legend, and a Jewish one this time, claims that it brought water to put out the fire in the Temple, which accounts not only for the red spots but the smoky plumage. It was connected with water and fertility; both Athene and Isis took its form.

The Chinese say that the Dragon is a symbol of fertility and that it likes eating swallows. If you should dare to do this and you cross water, the dragon will rise up and eat you. An offering to the genie of the house used to be made throughout China, when the birds returned from the south. This was to procure the fertility of the women and according to the *Folklore of Birds* by Edward Armstrong, the ancestress of the Shang dynasty swallowed the egg of a swallow, which made her pregnant. "The modern form of the character for "sacrifice" corresponds to "spirit" plus "swallow on its nest".

In some places in Europe, a swallow which flew into a house would be smeared with oil and set free, taking the problems and sins of the house with it. A young bird was supposed to have a stone in its belly and if you found it on or before the August full moon, it could cure epilepsy and sometimes, blindness.

The swallow herb, which is the greater celandine, *Chelidonium majus* was given its name because it flowers with the coming of the swallow or because the mother swallow gives it to her brood to give them sight. *Cheledonion* is the Greek for swallow and Gerard says that *"The juice is good to sharpen the sight"*.

The next section is about hares and from the same song as "I shall get me into an hare" are the lines:-

> "I shall go into a bee, with mickle horror and dread of thee
> And flit to hive in the devil's name ere that I be fetched home
> Bee take heed of swallow hen, will harry thee close
> Both butt and ben."

Nightingale

This is another migrant bird. The males arrive about ten days before the females and their incessant song is to attract a mate. They are just as likely to sing during the day as at night, but the best time to hear them is at dusk on a warm late spring evening.

The song is truly unforgettable. In the *AA Book of British Birds* it is described thus. *"A rapid succession of repeated notes - some harsh, some liquid - including a very loud 'chooc-chooc-chooc' and a fluting, pleading 'pioo', building up slowly to a crescendo."*

Few people have ever seen this bird because it is very shy and only its song is heard. And heard it is. I was born in Kent and there were times when the noise of several males made one think unkindly of this lovely music. Then when I went to college the bally things seemed to follow me and they sang all night round the building.

The female lays five eggs which are olive or dark olive green and very protected. The nest is built close to the ground in dense undergrowth. It feeds on insects, earthworms, spiders and some berries.

There was a poem written by John of Guildford early in the 12th century which was secular in the extreme. It was later given a more pious rendering.

> *"With dolorous songs funeral,*
> *Some to sing and some to say*
> *Some to weep and some to pray."*

This is about the death of Cock Robin which seems to have been originally, a song about the death of an early medieval Don Juan.

It was called the "barley bird" in East Anglia because it arrived as the barley was sown, which probably makes it a fertility symbol.

The church, of course, made much of this continuous song as illustrating how prayer should perpetually ascend to God. It ain't always well received though.

A Greek poet complained

> *"Leaf-loving nightingales, loquacious sex,*
> *Sleep quietly, I beg, and cease your din."*

St. Cainnic bid the noisy birds of El Inish to hold their peace and Edward the Confessor is supposed to have complained that the song of the nightingale interrupted his devotions. It certainly interrupted my own studies and those of my fellow undergrads.

There is a legend that the nightingale and the blind worm used to have one eye each. The nightingale stole that of the blindworm to attend a fairy wedding and the blindworm vowed to steal it back, which is why the bally bird sings all night. Alternatively, he sings to compensate the worm.

In the *"Conference of Birds"* by Farid ud-din Attar the nightingale is greeted thusly:-

"Salutations, Oh Nightingale of the Garden of Love. Utter your plaintive notes caused by the wounds and pains of love. Lament sweetly from the heart."

108

It goes on for a long time, but that is the gist. It is a fascinating book and well worth reading.

The Ancient Greeks thought that if the flesh of the ever wakeful nightingale was eaten, sleep would be difficult.

March Hares

"All things that love the Sun are out of doors,
The tky rejoices at the morning's birth.
The grass is bright with raindrops, on the moors
The hare is running races in her mirth."

Wordsworth

The animal most associated with March and with witches, is the hare. A lovely, gentle creature, loving to her offspring and very playful. It used to be thought that male hares boxed each other to win a female, but this is not so. Female hares do the boxing, fending off importunate males until they are ready to mate. They were called "puss" because of their habit of washing like a cat.

A Witch and a Hare

It used to be thought that witches turned themselves into hares to escape their pursuers. If the hare was wounded, the witch would bear the wound next day. They did the same thing to travel secretly to their coven moots. This, presumably, was when it was too dangerous to fly on their broomsticks or ragwort stalks.

When witches were about their shape-changing they were said to chant the following old rhyme:-

> "Hare, hare, God send thee care,
> I am in hare's likeness now;
> But I shall be a woman even now.
> Hare, hare. God send thee care."

There was also the song, part of which I quoted in the section on the Swallow

> "I will get me into an hare
> With sorrow and sighing and mickle care,
> And I shall go in the Devil's name
> Aye, til I come home again.

It seems to be quite clear that no actual transformation was attempted, or indeed was considered. The witch merely acted the movements of the creatures she called, and that she imitated the actions of both the hunter and the hunted. She was a greyhound hunting the hare; the otter chasing the trout; the swallow catching the bee; and the cat tormenting the mouse.

I used to work for an old man who owned a large shooting estate in Essex. Occasionally, because of damage to crops he had to organise a shoot of hares. They can cause a lot of damage to cereal crops if their numbers get out of hand. He was always very reluctant to do this because he said that, when shot, they cried like babies. He had been in the Royal Navy for many years and was not a sentimental man but there were tears in his eyes as he told me this.

A few years ago I was on my way home from Essex and decided to make my usual visit to Avebury on the way. As I drove round the narrow lanes, I always avoid motorways if I can, I was thinking about my life and wondering if I was kidding myself about my real attachment to working for the Earth.

It was a lovely evening and the corn had just been harvested, so the straw was still lying in the fields. I slowed down near an open gate and looked through it to the fields beyond. As I watched, a sizeable hare loped through the gate, looked at the car and began to trot up the lane in front of me. About thirty yards further on there was another gate, opening onto another field on the other side of the lane. She turned in here and then faced me. I stopped the car, turned off the engine and we watched one another for a minute or so.

Then I said "Oh, Wise one, am I fooling myself? Am I doing the right thing?" She looked at me for some time. Her eyes were a calm amber and her black-bordered ears twitched as if she was growing impatient. Then she nodded, stamped her foot and trotted off across the field.

I don't know if hares nod nor if they get impatient and stamp, but she seemed to do both. Afterwards, I felt that yes, I was doing the right work for me. Going to Avebury only confirmed this. I found a book about these lovely creatures which I treasure to this day.

The hare was a corn spirit. Each year we do a rite which embodies the old rite of Cutting the Hare. When most of the corn has been reaped, a stook, as we used to call it when I was young, was left standing; this you understand was when most reaping was done

111

by hand. The reapers, both men and women encircled it and dropped back to widen the circle. Then each threw the sickle until the "hare' was cut down. We tie a red ribbon round it to signify the death of the corn spirit. It must be cut below the knot. Then the 'hare ' is carried to a natural altar and blessed with milk and water and sometimes with honey. It should be placed over the kitchen door of the farmhouse. I keep mine on a shelf until the next sowing, when it goes out into the cornfield.

We do have a variation on this, but more of that in the chapter on the Autumnal Equinox.

Two Love Spells for the Vernal Equinox

> "If your love to you you'd bring
> Hold these in your hand in Spring.
> Myrtle green and violets blue
> Then will your love come to you."

Also

> "Of violets and lavender, take each a few,
> Enclose them with myrtle of dark green hue
> Make them in a posy, small and round and bright,
> You will see your true love in your dreams tonight."

This is an old charm to Honour a Tree at the Vernal Equinox

> "When nights and days are balanced and halved
> Cut from the branches March has saved
> Twelve supple wands all budded green
> Twist them together to weave a crown.
>
> Summer will come, and the winter wind
> Turning and turning the leaves on their stems

112

Then they must fall, but now in Spring
The twig is bound, but the bud remains.

Hang the leaf from a sturdy limb
Of Oak or Maple, or Ash or Elm,
Thus will the tree live long and well.

This came from a very old book but who the author was, I do not know. The cover was gone and the paper was brittle, so if anyone knows who wrote it, I would be very glad to hear from them.

A Talisman for Wealth

For gains of money, work to Jupiter and on Thursday. Burn light blue or rich purple candles and make your talisman on tin, the metal of Jupiter. The incenses of Jupiter are rich ones, Frankincense, Ambergris and Saffron, use these with some blue incense made of violets, roses, cedar and orris, with the seeds of Ash and some nutmeg grated in. You can use benzoin and grains of paradise but you can make a good one with far more easily obtained materials.

Have four light blue candles, two green and one yellow. Light the blue ones saying:-

> *"These candles are dedicated to Jupiter for the Higher Gain of myself."*

Light the two green ones and say;-

> *"These candles are dedicated to Venus for the Lesser Gain of myself."*

Light the yellow candle and say:-

> *""May my wish be taken to Mercury on the smoke of this candle."*

Then circle the altar three times and at each pass sprinkle incense on the burner, saying:-

> "By Jupiter, Venus and Mercury, I light my candles in
>   colours three.
> For gain for my hearth and family. As I will so may it be.
> I ask no very large amount, but just enough for me to count
> For paying to all what I owe, As I will, may it be so."

Make a talisman in either tin or copper for Venus. Use their signs and your own birth sign and the sign for gain. If the spell has been written down, burn it on the incense and allow the candles to burn down. When all is finished take the scraps into the garden and let them fly into the wind.

By the way, don't try using Mercury; it is poisonous once it gets into the air. It becomes Mercuric Oxide which won't do you a scrap of good.

The Tarot card is the Moon and this is the time of the very high Spring tides. The Moon is concerned with Kharmic destiny, what the Anglo-Saxons called 'weird'. It is also about debts, with ESP and with extreme sensitivity. This is a good time to recall past lives but only if you have two people you can trust with you.

Now, I do not know where the above came from. I have no recollection of writing it myself. I rather think that the woman who edited the original edition must have included it. She certainly left out a lot and made some very strange additions. Coming as it does on the 21st March or thereabouts, the Equinox is just in Pisces, which is ruled by the Moon and Neptune.

Never try to Astral travel or do anything with past lives by yourself. It can be frightening and not at all a happy experience. Many women would love to think that they were Cleopatra or some other great and powerful queen. This is not a thing to be desired. They died rather nasty deaths for one thing and it is more than a little presumptuous for another. Remember that the possibility that we all died peacefully in our beds is remote. Considering the history of the human race, it is more probable that we died from some revolting disease or that we were slaughtered after a battle and those are the good ones. Leave this aspect of the craft well alone unless you are really experienced.

When people tell me that they were great high priests or priestesses of Chaldea, Atlantis, Egypt or Greece, I take it with a very large pinch of salt and say "Oh. I was building the stone circles then".

Now, I know what you are going to say. Why has she been babbling on about swallows and nightingales when everyone knows that the harbinger of Spring is the Cuckoo. Well, it ain't. Spring begins, as you know, at Imbolc, not the Vernal Equinox, and anyway, the Cuckoo doesn't arrive until latish April. But anyway, here goes.

The Cuckoo

I do not know if it still happens, but once upon a time the letter page of the Times was inundated every April by "Incredulous" of Chichester; "Astounded" from Tunbridge Wells, not to mention "An Enquirer" from Epsom, all asking the same thing - "I have just hear the first cuckoo. Is this a record?" The answer was usually "No, someone else had heard it last week".

If you have been idle, the first time you hear the call could mean an early death. It means the same thing if you hear it in bed. They say "Lazy bird, lazy man." There is another side to this, however. This is a bird of augury and it spends so much time answering questions that it has no time to build a nest, which is why it always used some other poor bird's.

If it flies over your head or lands on a dead branch, that also is a sign of an early demise. Even the direction of the sound is significant. From the right it is lucky and obviously from the left it is unlucky. From the North, it is disaster from the South "it will be a good butter year".

You must turn over the coins in your pocket when you first hear it. In Scotland it is called *"eun sidhe"* the Bird of the Fairies. It was thought that it spent the winter in the round barrows, which we all know, are the entrances to the Otherworld.

In Berkshire, it was called the Pent cuckoo when it was captured and penned to maintain the fertility of Spring. There is a merrie tale of the Wise Men of Gotham, circa 1630, which I am sure you are dying to hear.

"On a time, the Wise Men of Gotham captured and penned a cuckoo to make her sing all the year round. They made a hedge, round in compass, in the middle of the town into which they put the cuckoo, to whom they said, "Sing here all the year round and ye shall lack neither meat nor drink" The cuckoo, as soon as she found herself encompassed, flew away, OVER the hedge.

"A vengeance on her," they cried *"We made not our hedge high enough".* Which goes to show that if you want to pen a cuckoo, make sure you put a lid on it.

One saying is that she arrives with the ripening barley and departs as soon as she hears the sickle, and before she lays her egg, she steals an egg from the host nest and holding it in her bill, flies off with it to a convenient branch to eat it.

> *"The Cuckoo is a pretty bird, she singeth as she flies.*
> *She bringeth us good tidings, she telleth us no lies.*
> *She sucketh little birds eggs to make her voice so clear*
> *And when she sings "Cuckoo" the summer draweth near."*

There is a version about her eating mud, which is supposed to drive away the rain, yet the call is supposed to foretell imminent rain.

On hearing the first call you should gather the earth from around your right foot. This is a strong flea repellent. And if you believe that....

Or...On hearing the first call, turn round three times on your left foot and you will find a hair the colour of your future husband's. This, from Mother Bunchs' Closet.

It is also unlucky to hear before breakfast (because you have stayed in bed) (see above) it is however, lucky to hear when out walking.

It is bad luck to hear it when you are hungry BUT a child born at the first call will always be lucky. HOWEVER if you hear it after Midsummer your partner will die.

In the ballad of Cock Robin the Cuckoo is the grave digger who "tolls from a crooked Birch."

In Hereford, it comes in time for Orleton Fair: "to buy a horse, then goes to Brom (Brompton Bryan) to sell it. On the Scottish border, it comes either on the 1st or 2nd of April by the old calender, the 12th or 13th by the Julian. In Devon it arrives in March. In Norfolk it arrives in April but everyone agrees that it changes its tune in June. when it sings "Cuck-clunk".

In Sussex, "if he stays until September, 'tis more than the oldest man can remember".

A medieval scribe wrote:-

> The cuckoo in his mantle grey cries all day from the tree tops
> And verily, God shield me still,
> Well speeds my quill beneath the copse.

Lethbridge tells the story of the old woman (the Cailleach) Goddess of Winter, who lets the bird out of the underworld in spring, thus associating her with Freya, Goddess of Spring and Fertility.

Enough of the folk lore. They seem to rest on standing stones, which makes the old country folk say that they are "hawks" for a time. It is supposed to fly in the same manner as a hawk, straight and level, moving the wings but little. The only ones I have seen in flight moved in a gentle wave-like motion; reminding me of the everlasting combers of the Indian Ocean. When flying it rarely rises above the tops of the highest trees, which in my young days used to be elms, which are sadly departed from the countryside now.

They rest on fence posts and when courting collect in small groups. They fly off but soon return. Several years ago, the B.B.C. made one of their splendid Wild Life series on the life of the cuckoo. I have never felt the same way about them since. The sight of that prehistoric monster heaving the eggs and hatchlings of the willow warblers out of the nest turned my stomach. I happen to like reed warblers.

Incidentally, the first one I ever saw flew across the lane as I cycled along it. It flew from my left to my right, cucking as it flew. That was when I was fourteen I am sixty-five now, so death if a little tardy, is slightly more expected.

Chapter Five

Beltaine

May Eve   30th April

The Rising of the Sun and the Running of the Deer

In the days when our magic was entirely seasonal, before the over-laying of the worship of the Sun, the Celebration of the Eve of the Beltaine Fires, literally the Fires of Bel, the Sky God (Welsh *tan*=fire) happened in this wise.

The Stag Lord, who had been elected at birth and now in his fourteenth year, ran with the deer. At some point, the Great Stag would scent an enemy or rival in the herd and would turn to see him off. The young hunter had to overcome the stag. There would be a substitute, in the event of the chosen one being wounded or even killed. This is problematical. Our ancestors were quite capable of cheating, of course, but they would have understood that a substitute would mean that the year would be disastrous.

No one could lead the tribe if he became disabled. Nuada of the Silver Arm is a case in point. He lost an arm fighting the Firbolg and had to give up his leadership. After seven years, the Gods made him a new silver one, decorated with runes. They had the technology.

So, when the victorious young Stag Lord, having slain the Great Stag, returned, with its antlers from the Running, he mated with the Maiden, who also had been chosen from birth. This union, for which they had been trained all their lives, was the Great Rite, in which the Goddess, represented by the Maiden and the God, in the person of the young Stag Lord, brought

fertility to the land for the summer. What she conceived was the following Spring.

This was extended later. At Avebury on May morning, the nubile young maidens walked in procession from the Sanctuary, along the Avenue, and from Beckhampton the young men came, also in procession. As the two groups reached the centre of the circle they paired off and presumably mated, the virgin blood of the maidens fertilising the land.

There are groups who go through this ceremony at the vernal equinox, which is alright I suppose, so long as they do not call themselves Oak Lords and May Maidens. The child of this union is called the Star Child of the Winter Solstice.

I find this difficult to understand. The Star Child had nothing to do with witchcraft or the Old Religion, being a Middle Eastern importation, first with Mithras of the Legions and then, I suppose, with Christianity. Although one can have a fight between the Light and the Dark at the Equinox, one cannot have a fight between the Oak and the Holly at that time for the simple reason that the Oak is not in leaf and indeed, is hardly showing a bud and is probably still wearing last years brown leaves. The May blossom has not begun to show on the Hawthorns, although the Blackthorn may still be in blossom.

By the end of April, all the principal actors are on the scene, the Hawthorn is in blossom, the Oak is in leaf and the Holly is looking a bit tired. There is another point to be made in this argument. At the Winter Solstice, the Great Goddess, as the Hag, has already gone down to the Otherworld, as we saw at Samhaine, so would not be around to give birth to this child. This is where the purely natural aspect of the Old Religion has become out of tune with the worship of the Sun. Herne, Hunter and Dark Aspect of the god, has had his work cut out protecting His children throughout the winter. Witchcraft is about common sense. The Gods must think that the Man Kind, although they sometimes try, especially something new, are very trying.

It used to be said that May is an unlucky month in which to be married. This superstition dates from the time the Christian

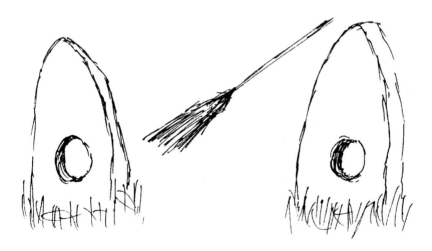

church was trying to suppress the Old Religion. May was always a month of sexual fun and games throughout Europe until the Reformation. After which, anyone decorating their homes with May blossom was likely to be taken up for a witch.

In olden times, men and women did not vow to be true to one another until death did them part. Ancient man was wise enough to know that this is not always possible. He probably did not know that every cell in the body is changed over seven years, so one was physically not the same person at all. I"m not sure that he bothered about the mental and spiritual bit.

So at a special place, be it a long barrow, a holed stone or a cromlech or simply over a broom, a couple would hand-fast themselves on May morning, pledging themselves for a year and a day after which they might choose to continue together or go their separate ways.

These arrangements were typical of matriarchal societies and there were no problems about the children of such unions. Children belonged to their tribes and their mothers and everything passed through the female line. In a matriarchy there is no such concept as illegitimacy, one always knows one's mother, of one's father one might be less sure. That stigma only arrived with patriarchy, when power switched dramatically from the female to the male line and every man decided that he needed to know his sons were his own.

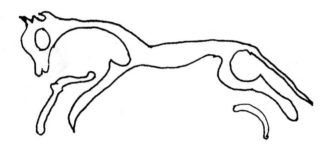

The Beltaine Rites

"Oh do not tell the priest of our plight, or he would call it a sin.
But we've been out in the woods all night a'conjuring summer in."

We gather the May blossom from a hedge bordering the road at
the bottom of the hill, but we need to find a tree closer to home, in
blossom, round which we can dance early in the morning. We used
to have a very old place in the bend of the river. Most conven-
iently, and rather strangely, there were concentric rings of trees;
with an old apple orchard, slightly off centre. These rings were
firstly, birch; then holly, then small oaks, then the orchard and
bordering the river willow and alder, who represent the Goddess
and Bran respectively. Right in the middle of the small orchard
was a very symbolic apple tree, half alive and half dead, showing
the two halves of the year. It still bears the remains of the
chaplets we left several years ago.

Each time we worked there we walked through wet fields with the
rain washing down our necks. We had prepared the site, removing
thistles, nettles and such logs as might trip us. We made a circle
of logs the first year which remained in place and only needed
clearing.

One had gone before and stood guard at the entrance to the circle.
He looked enormous, clad in black leather and crowned with a
superb set of antlers, very much Herne, Lord of the Holly. He
challenged our right to enter and announced His names and
titles. He demanded to know who would fight him for the hand of
the Maiden. The Oak Lord, new to the part and appaled by the
sight of this huge opponent lost his nerve and ran away. This was
a little upsetting but nothing we could say would make him face
that very alarming figure, even the knowledge that if he failed to
do his part, there would be no summer and no harvest. Eventually, we had to choose another Oak Lord and the poor chap
trailed miserably home, never to be seen again.

Another year, my two sons played the parts. Both had good lines
in flannel and ad libbed beautifully. Now remember, I said that

the willows bordered a fast flowing, rather deep river. On this occasion the bank was particularly slippery after much rain. As brothers do, the fight became realistic and ignoring our horrified yells, our heroes slid, not very gracefully, into the water. That put a fairly conclusive end to the fight.

We fished them out and as we were all so wet anyway, finished the ritual and then squelched home to showers and breakfast.

On another occasion, as we returned for the morning rite I was chatting to someone walking just behind me. Hearing stifled giggles from further back I turned, only to find that I was being escorted by two old farm horses. The field was part of an equine retirement home They seemed to know what was going on, for they and several others, came all the way to the orchard and stood outside the circle. At the end of the rite, they accompanied us back to the stile - they too, had welcomed the somewhat dripping summer in.

Most of the games we play now were thought of then, all those years ago. I had never heard of Gardner or Saunders and had no idea that others were preserving the old ways. We still do this rite in several parts. The fighting bit is usually done in my back garden, or over the fence in the field. After the rite we say goodbye to the Holly, the Lord Herne, who after all this exercise, returns to the Wild Wood to rest until he is recalled at Samhaine. We welcome the Goddess, who is now the Mother to be, who will be with us throughout the summer.

MAY DAY, the First Day of Summer

At one time, May morning was greeted all over Europe with a foot stamping dance. The ONE-two-three rhythm woke the Earth up ready for summer. In Cornwall they still do this; perhaps that is why they have better summers than the rest of Britain.

Following the old ways, we go out early and find our specially chosen Hawthorn, the one that has most blossom. Wearing our chaplets of flowers we dance round it and sing the summer in. We have a piper and a drummer and we sing all the way there and back again.

One year, a great group of people from many parts of the country gathered at one of the larger long barrows. We duly did our thing and then trooped a mile to lay our chaplets and bunches of flowers, May blossom, Apple blossom and bluebells on the great White Horse, only to find someone had beaten us to it. The Horse was already covered so we added ours and left.

The Midday Rite

On the surface, this appears to be a series of games, but each one is ancient and has far more meaning than any modern rite, however well staged and equipped it might be. One lady informed me that she hadn't time to play but that she would come to the "proper" rite, when we did it.

Once again, each person taking part is expected to bring something to give away. Remember that all through the year, we have to cut away the things we no longer need. We always advise anyone taking part to make comprehensive notes about how he felt before, during and after. This should include any dream that might provide added illumination or inspiration.

Down by the great oak tree, (when I first wrote this book we did this rite beneath an oak, now we do it in yet another orchard, round a pear tree, all the apple trees being on a steep slope and protected by walls of bramble). The Bel fires have already been lit. Singing, we begin the rite by running between the fires, casting away that which we no longer need and calling a blessing upon the Earth as we go. We ask another blessing on all we will do throughout the summer months. Somehow I seem to have written the words "Everyone is blessed with dew".

(I suppose I wrote it, but at mid-day on the 1st May, it is difficult to find much dew, there might be rain however. I think the editor put in another four pen'th.

We welcome the four elements, picturing them as the gentle things of Earth. The Wind in the trees, the sweet smell of Hawthorn and Elder and the sight of the birds drifting on currents of Air. In the South we give thanks for the fires that have warmed us and those that destroy unwanted influences or belongings. Water is found in the springs in which this part of the country abounds, the rain and the dew.

And for the Earth, everything that grows upon the land and the creatures now bringing forth their young. This is the most important blessing of this time. Beltaine is all about fertility.

Beltaine Games

Hundreds of years ago, the men of the tribe would hunt many creatures to both prove their manhood and feed the tribe. One of the most ferocious of these was the Wild Boar, it could kill any man on foot. Actually, it was only necessary for them to hunt a couple of days a week. The women, however, were constantly engaged in finding berries, fruit, nuts and herbs, this they did every day. There are no wild boar left in Britain, few men are successful hunters so our men hunt the Wild Boar Sausage. This is a passive beast, not in the least dangerous, so the children join in this hunt.

One of the fleeter men carrying a bunch of these objects is given a good start and then the fellers chase him. While this is going on, the women have been doing their thing round the fires, and have arranged oat cakes, mead, wine, cider and beer, flowers and fruit between the fires. As they complete each circle they jump over the food and say "*I am formed in beauty, in love and in power.*" then they continue circling and each time they jump they say something about the elements. "Water is wet"; "the Sun is Hot"; "Fire Burns" and anything else they can think of.

By this time the men have returned; they are cheered for being such brave little soldiers and re-join the circle. Each man is led through the fires by each woman and they are also expected to say something relevant. The women take the wine and cakes to one fire and the men take the sausages and beer to the other, they give thanks to the God and Goddess, then once more they all run between the fires.

Hoop anò Ball

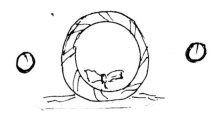

The meaning of this game is lost in antiquity. It should be played with a large hoop, bound round with ribbons and decorated with flowers. There are two smallish balls - gold and silver.

One source says that these represent the God and Goddess and are a straightforward fertility symbol. Another says they are the Sun and Moon passing through the heavens.

Two people hold the hoop, and two others stand on either side. They each throw their ball through the hoop at the same time.

It is unlucky not to make a clean catch, and very unlucky to drop the ball or fail to get it through the hoop. When everyone has made a clean throw and catch the balls are thrown as far away as possible by the last man, and the last woman hangs the hoop on the tree. We end this game by playing an even older one - Passing the Jug and Eating the Sausage. There are songs, for this part of the rite cannot be done in silence. We used to have a stream to jump over, but now we use a large bowl or puddle. We do this to give thanks for water and to ensure that there is enough to feed the land and crops during the coming months. It should always be remembered that plants CAN grow without the Sun, providing there is light but they cannot grow without water.

Perhaps we do this a little too effectively, given the nature of English summer weather.

The May Tree

Everyone should have brought about twenty yards of ribbon with them. One end of which is attached to a garland placed as high on the trunk of the tree as the tallest man can manage. This is the famous Weaving Dance. This is done every year and so should be quite well known. BUT NO.

We start off well enough. Man and woman round the circle, each holding the loose end of his own ribbon. Men turn left and women right, so that the women are going widdershins and the men deosil. They know that they must pass first right and then left, ducking under a ribbon or taking it over the top in turn. It sounds so easy, doesn't it. We should end up with a nice tidy plait as we weave summer, warmth and growth into the tree. But although everyone dances with ferocious concentration, there is always a muddle, especially as some people have shorter ribbons than others and get wound into the weave.

Heigh Ho! Get them out and tie the ends. Finally, we all join hands and dance for as long as we have breath to the ONE-two-three rhythm.

We did try putting a tape cassette in the branches of the tree, but it was too quiet to hear. Mine is a decorous, small machine not a ghetto blaster. We have had an assortment of musical instruments to play the tune, from dulcimers and harps to drums and penny whistles, that year we had no one to play and we got breathless very quickly.

One of the chants we sing goes:-

"Beltaine fires we sing, we sing
With this poppet, health I bring.
To one who pines in pain and sorrow
Beltaine fires, heal her tomorrow.

Oak and May we come to greet
Merry here again we meet.
May all who pine in pain and sorrow
By Oak and May be healed tomorrow.

Oak and May and Beltaine fire
In those we know but one desire,
May all good people on the Earth
Come to Life, and Health and Mirth."

(Of course, you could go into complete
doggerel and the last couplet becomes

Earth and all that's sick here in it
Be cured of woe this very minnit.)

The Beltaine Tree

The Oak, Hawthorn and Holly
are most important at this
season. The Holly, having
done His stint during Winter
and lost the fight for the hand
of the Maiden last evening,
goes back into the greenwood.
This is actually what happens. The Holly stands out clearly when
all other trees are bare of leaves but once the Hazel, Elder,
Sycamore, Rowan, Blackthorn, Hawthorn and Oak begin to put on
their new leaves, it blends back into the mass of colour. Our
ancestors were not stupid when they said he goes back into the
forest.

129

The Oak has long been associated with the Gods of Thunder and in the days when people had sun blinds at their windows, the pulls were nearly always tipped with carved wooden acorns, which were supposed to protect the house from lightning.

Any Oak struck by lightning was considered to be particularly blessed. People would travel miles to take a piece of such a tree as a great protective talisman, despite all the gruesome stories of "ye olde oake on the blarsted 'eath".

The Druids are said to have taken their name from this tree. Certainly they worshipped in oak groves (not stone circles) which the invading Romans deliberately cut down in an attempt to undermine the priests' power. The old cheer "*Hip, Hip Hooray*" was originally part of a Druid chant to the Oak as was "*Hey, Nonny Nonny*".

In the story of the Battle of the Trees, fought against the Man Kind, Bran the Blessed, whose tree was the Alder, led the trees. Man was led by Gwydion, whose symbol was the Oak. It seems a pity that the trees lost. The Oak was called the Guardian of the Door and it unlikely to be a coincidence that the great doors of castles and churches were made of oak. As Guardians, of course, they were "The Wooden Walls of England" meaning the ships of the Royal Navy, Hearts of Oak and all that.

Dreaming of a great, healthy oak tree was considered to be very lucky. If acorns grew on it, the dream foretold of children who would cause their parents to be very proud of them. Descending into utter doggerel again for this I came up with

> "*To promise a man a dream of an Oak which grows both hale and hearty*
> *Is to promise him sons to make him proud,*
> *Who will come to the aid of the party.*"

I do apologise, I was never a poet. William Hope McGonnegal and I make a good pair. Mine, however are mercifully short.

130

The Trees of the Goddess

We have a choice here between the Willow and the Hawthorn. The graceful Willow brings luck in love and the May has ancient links with fertility. It was associated with the Roman cult of Flora, Goddess of Spring, whose rather wild May Day festival was called the Floralia, and no doubt, shocked those austere Roman matrons no end.

The Willow, (*salix alba*) is however dedicated to the Moon and Water, and has further dedications to Hecate and Artemis. It does have one to Persephone, who, as the Maiden has just been impregnated. I think we will leave the willow until a later time.

Hawthorn
Crataegus oxyacantha
Uath

The Ancient Greeks propitiated the equally ancient Goddess within the tree with five torches made from hawthorn wood. I would have supposed this to make Her a little more than somewhat annoyed, although She does not object to burning quite so much as the Elder, in whom our Goddess dwells as the Hag. After this incineration, the Greeks, a pragmatic race, settled down to feasting and drinking and probably smashing plates a lot.

The Athenian maidens decorated the altar of Hymen with the flowers and carried hawthorn branches at the weddings of their friends. As a symbol of Hope?

One of the country names of this tree is the Tree of Chastity, a misnomer one would think considering all the fun and games surrounding Beltaine.

I did mention that the Tarot card is the Lovers. It would be an interesting subject for discussion. Can Lovers be chaste? Perhaps as another symbol of Hope.

131

We used to call it Bread and Cheese when I was little, the leaves were supposed to taste of this delightful supper dish. It was the custom in Norfolk until the beginning of this century, which usually means until the first World War for any servant who could bring in a branch of hawthorn in full blossom on the 1st of May to receive a dish of cream for breakfast. The farmers are usually safe. It is difficult to find such a branch now. The tree is usually in full flower by the 11th May, Old May Day.

Walter de la Mare in his poem *"The Hawthorn Hath a Deathly Smell"* says:-

"the silver of the May wreathed is with incense for
The Judgement Day."

You can dry the petals for pot pourri and they make a delicious, light flavoured jelly.

The blossom is very important to many insects, including hover flies, which reward the tree by pollinating the blossom. The berries are incredibly useful. They make a medicine par excellence for those suffering from high blood pressure which is very easy to make. Simply put as many berries as you can gather into a large saucepan, cover with water and simmer for several hours, making sure to keep enough water to drain off. Having done this mix with some honey to taste, take a spoonful three times a day. It has an effect on the platelets of the blood which prevents them from sticking together, which in turn, prevents blood clots forming.

Keep a good lot back to make Hawthorn wine, which is a bit like pink champagne and much nicer than an ordinary Rosé. This is made by the usual method, which you can find in any book on the subject, but do be careful how you store it - it has been known to explode.

Beltaine Flower

Ladies Smock
Carmendine pratensis

This is a delicate little plant, found in riverside meadows at this time of the year. Dedicated to the Lady, it is very apt, I think. When I had my dog, one of my delights was to find the first one in late Spring. It was usually the first time one could sit on the grass and listen to the growth of the Earth.

It is also known as the Cuckoo Flower, probably because the wretched bird arrives at the same time. There are two versions of the origin of the name.

The first, pretty one, to the poet's eye, as it were, is that although the flower is either pale mauve or pink, the patches on a meadow look like the white smocks of ladies, spread out on the grass to bleach in the sun. This is what people used to do, long before they had washing lines or tumble dryers, the clothes were draped over brambles or the grass. In *"Love's Labour Lost"* Shakespeare wrote:-

> *"When daisies pied and violets blue **
> *And Ladies Smocks all silver white,*
> *And Cuckoo-buds of yellow hue*
> *Do paint the meadows with delight."*

* (although he wrote 'blew')

and later

> *"When turtles tread, and rooks, and daws,*
> *And maidens bleach their summer smocks."*

The second, rather earthier, not so poetical version which I gained from Ron Freethys' splendid book, *"Agar to Zenry"*, is that it comes from an Olde Englishe word meaning "a lecherous glance". and as it was used in many of the more down to earth May Day celebrations, it would appear that though the smocks in question were spread on the grass, they might have contained the maiden, in the loosest possible sense.

An anonymous Irish poem, dating from the 15th century has it:-

> *"Tender cress and cuckoo flower,*
> *And curly-haired fair-headed maids,*
> *Sweet was the sound of their singing."*

Be that as it may, the flowers are rich in iron and magnesium, and Vitamin C. They could be eaten in salads. Dried, they were used to treat epilepsy in the 18th and 19th centuries. Culpeper says that it can be used against scurvy, to promote urine, break the stone, restore lost appetite and help the digestion.

The plant also gets rid of vermin and was one of the favoured Druid herbs.

There would have to be a reference to Mary. It seems that it was the smock she was wearing when Jesus was born. She left it behind when the family fled to Egypt and it was later found by St. Helena and was taken to St. Sophia in Byzantium. Even later it was stolen by Charlemagne and taken to Aix-la-Chapelle, where it was worshipped as a relic. Quite why it comes to be spread about English meadows I can't think, but as the man says, you pays your money and you takes your choice.

Beltaine Herb

Dill
Anethum graveolens

The main thing to remember about this herb is never grow it within thirty feet of fennel. They are very closely connected and will cross pollinate, thus giving you a herb which tastes of neither.

By itself it is rich and aromatic. The name comes from the old Norse "dilla" which means to "lull" a baby, as in lullaby. It was always used in gripe water, which I loved to drink when my sisters bought it for their babies. It was supposed to "lull' the little mites into a more tranquil mood. Perhaps I took too much, it never did the same for me. Romany girls used to eat lots of this herb when they were pregnant because it had the reputation of stimulating milk production.

In earlier times, when people had to go to church on pain of paying a shilling fine if they didn't; the smell of the great unwashed was kept from the delicate nostrils of the wealthy by the simple expedient of chewing the seeds. They also used it to stay off the pangs of hunger caused by sermons of inordinate length and crashing boredom, droned at them before breakfast.

It is very helpful to people who have high blood pressure and are on a low salt diet as it contains many mineral salts which are gentle on the system.

Dill goes well with cucumber especially, and can be added to mashed potatoes, trout (instead of fennel) and tomatoes (instead of Basil) and chicken.

This herb also puts witches to flight, and is added to love potions.

The Beltaine Animal

Pigs used to be fed on beech mast and acorns and so belong to the oak by association. Even in the days of the royal forests, when the local population were kept out of the woods because they not only might, but would poach the deer, there were laws of pannage, which allowed them to run their pigs freely, to  eat up the fallen nuts. This was a way of keeping the undergrowth down, and preventing the growth of too many saplings. Although there was a great market for wood, those who had been given large tracks of land managed to keep the price up, by keeping the supply down.

The Pig is a powerful Goddess totem but please do not think of it as a sort of fluffy bunny creature. Sows in farrow are dangerous beasts; sows with young are even more so and boars are dangerous whatever the time of year.

There is a tendency among those who practise Wicca and even the much older witchcraft, to think of the animals which are used as totems as things to be 'summoned up' and treated with scant respect. Do not do this. Most of the wild things thought of as totems are potentially very dangerous beasts and are not nearly so tame as one would like to think. Try standing in a stable with a stroppy mare, you'll find out.

I have the horrors when visiting a circle of people I do not know very well, and hear some arrogant idiot "Summon, stir and call up" not only Eagles, Bears, Wolves, Bulls, Cows, but Lions, and Men, the most dangerous creature of them all.

The one that really worries me though, is the Boar. Most of the above come from ritual magic, or Middle Eastern magic of some kind. But the Boar, my loves, is not from Celtic, or Scots or Pict. It goes back to the very earliest hunters, to the time of impenetrable primeval forest, when the Man kind, hunting the fairly inoffensive deer suddenly heard a crashing in the undergrowth and was faced with the fastest, most ferocious and intelligent of all wild things. This intelligence was not tamed and has never been tamed. It is pure chaos and is designed to kill because something is there to kill. These hunters had spears, possibly sharpened in the fire but although these might have been backed up with slings, they probably did not yet have the bow and arrow.

Their knives would have been of flint, good for skinning a carcass, but not much good against a hide as thick as that of the boar with a thick layer of protecting bristles.

If someone managed to wound this charging fury this made the matter worse. There is little so thoroughly savage as a wounded boar.

So the people who took the Boar as a totem did it with honour and respect and not a little fear. It was the first totem of hunting man because it was the one that frightened him most. Thousands of years before his imagination developed enough to make Gods unto himself; thousands of years before he settled down to become a farmer, thousands of years before he began to build stone circles and long barrows, he honoured and respected the boar.

So do not summon him. If you need his strength, and you'd much better not, ask politely and even then you might regret it. A boar charging round your circle could cause more trouble than you could handle in a lifetime.

But back to the pig. Apart from being the MOST intelligent domesticated creature it has the great distinction of never fouling its sleeping quarters. Anyone who says "dirty pig" has no idea how wrong they are. They rarely get lousy as do most other animals.

They can smell the wind and when they run about with straw in their mouths they signal windy weather to come.

Old country lore says that they should only be killed when the Moon is waxing or the meat will shrink when it is cooked. Judging by the way they are killed these days, every joint must be half its original size. My own grandfather said that they should never be killed on a Monday which is sacred to the Moon.

Pigs were "protected" from witches on May morning. Little crosses of birch and rowan were put over their sties to keep them safe. Granddad used to do this too, and it was from his family that I learned my witchcraft.

Beltaine Symbols

May Day falls in Taurus which is the fixed Earth sign, ruled by both Venus and the Moon. With those two ladies and the Bull, it reeks of fertility all round. Its colour is orange and the gem is Topaz.

It is associated with the Egyptian god, Osiris the King, and Hathor the fertile Cow, and She can be pretty dangerous too.

The tarot card is the High Priest, which expects not only physical fertility but fertility of the mind. From now on we are expected to grow every way.

To Sum up May Day, the rite of May Eve is the time of the fight between the Holly Lord, the Dark Lord of Winter, who is also the Stag of Seven Tines and Herne of the Wild Hunt and his other half, the Oak Lord, Sun King who is also a Stag, for the hand of the Maiden, who after conceiving the Spring becomes the Mother, the Goddess after her wedding night.

The Horned God is a Janus figure, the God Looking Both Ways. The Holly Lord, with all His other titles who has protected and watched over us during the winter months, fights Himself and becomes the Father, the Laughing God of the Greenwood who performs the same function during the summer. Remember, that the old ones had only two seasons.

In the same way, the Maiden who came back from the Under-world at Imbolc becomes the impregnated Mother, after Her night with the Oak Lord. she will later become the Crone who returns to the Underworld of the Dark Goddess of Death and Re-birth at Samhaine. Its all rather confusing really, as Spike Milligan used to say, but it becomes simple when you get used to it.

May Day Chants

This one should be chanted on the way to the early morning rite:-

Holly, Oak and Hawthorn, Hip, Hip Hooray,
Round we go to greet our Maiden on this May Day.

A general May Day Blessing

Oak and May
Upon this day
Will both heed
Those in need.

An Esbat Chant

On the night when the Moon is full
To the Esbat we hear the call
To come, to dance, to sing that all
May be strong and free and tall.
Round the circle dance by three

So our Goddess we may see;
In Her light our rite we do
To dedicate ourselves to You.

Spells

To Cure a Sty

An old cure for a sty at the corner of
the eye was to stroke it with the tail of
a tortoiseshell cat, still attached - one
presumes. This is only effective in the
month of May. While stroking you
should say:-

"I poke thee, I don't poke thee
I poke the queff that's under thee,
O Qualway... O Qualway."

I have never found out what that
means, but it is supposed to work.

For General Health and Happiness

Oak is the sun Lord, Maiden is the May
Take away our pains and woes on this May Day.
Oak is the Sun Lord, He will give us strength
He will take away our fears for the summer's length

Hawthorn is the Maiden, She will bring us peace
From the woes of aching hearts, She will bring release.
Oak Lord and maiden, Hip. Hip Hooray
Sing we and chant them on this May Day.

140

Chapter Six

The Summer Solstice and Midsummer

21st & 24th June

Let us start this chapter with a spell, for a change. It is quite long and anonymous. No one knows when it was written but, if the language is anything to go by, it is not very old by the standards used for spells.

"When June is ripe and days are full,
And Summer comes early to claim His throne
Walk before dawn to a silent height
And set three stones in an Eastern line.
Stand behind them while His light
Is rising over the distant land.
When He is in the Eastern sky
Offer these words and understand

"Sun of the Year, I move the Earth
To greet Thy sign, and set myself
To honour Thee in Earth's design."

Perfect the stones to mark His face
Follow their shadow twelve short paces
Pluck some leaf for an amulet
And wear on your coat let you forget.

Today is the longest day of the year. The Sun rises sometime between 03.53 and 04.43a.m. and sets between 20.31 and 21.22 p.m. BST. The Sun rises and sets at these times for three days, one before the solstice and one after. At least it seems like this, the difference in time being less than a second and not large enough to show on an ordinary clock. It no doubt shows on those at the Greenwich Observatory but only in micro-seconds.

From today the days get shorter and by obvious conclusion the nights get longer. The year will have turned once again and there is a slight feeling of sadness that we have seen the best of summer. This however, is not the case. As the hardest weather of winter usually comes after the winter Solstice, so the best of summer comes after this one.

It always surprises me that people actually think that summer begins with the solstice but will happily talk about Midsummer day, three days afterwards. This is due to brainwashing by those who would not admit the importance of May Day. There are two festivals, as there are two at the other end of the year the solstice and Midwinter.

I know that the English climate is a little odd but even we have longer that six days of summer. Not all at once perhaps, but scattered around between the showers.

The best known festival was, until recently, that of the Druids at Stonehenge. May I repeat that the Druids did not worship in stone circles but in Oak groves, so this well-known and ancient festival is modern. I used to go to these ceremonies, had done for about thirty-five years, and also stopped at the stones every time I happened to go past, which was about eight times a year. I got to know the old custodian well, we corresponded until his death. He had been there since before the 39-45 war, when he did have time off to be in the infantry. He was convinced, as I am, that the Sun has NEVER risen over the Heel Stone, not in 5,000 years. It rises well to the North and when it has been up for about three quarters of an hour touches the tip of the stone.

There is the added problem that almost every time I have been there there has been a thick layer of cloud over those Eastern hills so that, by the time you actually see the Sun it has been risen for a long time and is well up into the sky.

I have never managed to hear what those lads in the white nighties say as they wander round from point to point, but one year a wag in the watching throng began to sing "*Here we go round the Mulberry Bush*" and thirty thousand people collapsed.

Even given the possibility that all those thousands of years ago the eastern horizon was higher, chalk although hard, does weather over time, there would probably have been a range of trees there and you still couldn't have seen it. I do not believe that it was a Sun Temple at all, I think it was a temple for studying a particular constellation, that of Auriga. This group has one special star, which was viewed in this part of the world rather as Sirius was viewed by the Egyptians.

Its name is Capella, the She Goat of Auriga the Chariot. This is the only one of the ten brightest stars that never sets in these latitudes of the Northern hemisphere.

Before the current nonsense at the henge, that is before it was taken over by English Heritage, I spent at least one night a month, sitting in the middle of the place and Capella actually seems to circle over the Henge, throughout the year. Just as a matter of interest, it is 41 light years from the Earth, its mass is three times that of the Sun and its diameter is sixteen times larger. It is a very complex system and is actually four stars, two binaries and their companions. I think that the henge was built to enable the priesthood to study this parti-

cular phenomenon. Anyway, Avebury is a far more important Solar site.

The really important sighting is the one at sunset on the Winter solstice, when the sun does set between the uprights of the Great Trilithon.

X   X   X   X

So, the sun has reached His peak of Light and Heat and after this day will dwindle. The great wheel goes on. After the celebrations of this night the Great Lord of the Sun will become the Questing Hero until Lughnasad, the Death of Light, when He becomes the sacrifice, John Barleycorn, in other words the Harvest. Lughnasad is the old name for the Christian feast of Lammas, the First Loaf. Lugh was the old name, I'm not really sure whether it was the Celtic name or not, for the Lord of Light. His earlier name was Bel.

He really does have a great many names, this God. Not quite as many as Jehovah, but all to do with the world of nature. He is Cernunnos, and we can see Him clearly in the ancient figure cut into the chalk hill at Cerne Abbas in Dorset. It is also pictured on the Gundestrup cauldron. He is Herne, a name which probably comes from the same root and is closely associated with Pan, possibly not etemologically, but they are both Lords of the Greenwood, Guardians and Friends of animals and can both cause panic. This fear is not so much terror as awe. Once upon a time it was possible to walk alone in our woods, even during the war this was so, but there are so many twisted people about that this delightful pastime is denied us. However, in the days when we could do this as you went further into the wood you might feel a little curl of disquiet growing in your solar plexus. Not terror, but awe; something might be watching you and you could not be sure what it was.

If you stayed still the feeling might grow but the very best thing to do was to think of the small creatures living in the wood and to remember the passage in the *"Wind in the Willows"* which every child should know, where Pan is discovered with the lost baby otter resting by His legs. If you listened carefully, then, you might have hear the sound of pipes. If you sat even more quietly, something might appear. The Greenwood is not just a place to walk through. It is a place to experience with all your senses and you can only do this in silence.

Herne is the Green Man, Arthur's Green Knight. He is also the Janus figure, the God looking both ways as the Lord of the Holly in Winter; the Master of the Hell Hounds, called Yell in Devon and Gabriel in other parts of the country. He becomes the Lord of the Oak in Summer, consort of the Maiden-Mother; and He is the Lord of the Sun, Lord of Light, Questing Knight and finally John Barleycorn the Sacrificed God.

The old Herm stones at crossroads were this Janus figure, they looked four ways though, keeping an eye on all travellers. In many ways they were Mercury-Hermes, who as you know, was specially concerned with those who travelled, pack men, carriers, tinkers and thieves. this must also include Highwaymen. I wonder how many commercial travellers think of the old Herm when they come to a crossroad? Perhaps they should all wear the talisman of the much later St. Christopher.

I have actually only seen one of these stones, set into a wall in a very ancient village in Kent, on an incredibly old crossroad. The village is Otford and this is the place where the real last stand of the Housecarls of Harold took place perhaps even the place where Harold was actually killed, not by an arrow through his eye, but through his breast. Yet the idea persists that it all happened at Battle. History does get so mixed up.

This has been quite a long diversion from the Summer solstice but relevant, nevertheless.

We celebrate this day with three rites, at daybreak, midday and sunset.

The dawn rite takes place on a hill from which
we can actually see the sun rise. This means a
long trek up the hill, and along the flat where
the racecourse is. We stand facing the East
and as the Sun rises over the horizon we shout
a greeting. We then hold hands and dance
round, this gives us a very effective circle. As
we do so we ask the Sun to bless the Earth
with light and warmth and bring the crops to a
good harvest.

We thank Bel for shining upon us and mourn
the fact that His strength will begin to wane.
We offer blessings on all the Elements, and ask
that the rain be warm and light, because not
only do the crops need it but the cricket season
is under way, so I ask a private blessing on the
matches to be played. We all want to get out of
the heavy clothes of winter and into something
less bulky.

This is of necessity a short rite; most people
have come before going to work and they need a decent breakfast,
It is amazing how hungry one can get when working early in the
morning.

Those who can, stay and we do another small rite at noon,
praising the Sun in His height. I'm told that the Druids do this at
Stonehenge and even to them it is a much more private affair.

The afternoon is spent preparing yet another site, looking towards
the West for the evening rite. We prepare the fires and try to

think where the flares should be sited
so that they have half a chance to
withstand the evening gales.

146

The Evening Solstice Rite

This is pretty formal and we do all the ritual magic stuff. We ask people to bring robes and especially flowers and fruit. I stress home produced stuff, grown here on the island, not oranges, pineapples or kiwi fruit. We want strawberries, cherries, raspberries and plums if we can be sure they are local. We like these chiefly because they are small and easily eaten. You don't have to stand around and watch people chewing large apples.

Several people go ahead of the main group; to make sure the fires and flares are lit. The cauldron has been set in the middle of the circle along with honey cake and some golden wine. Actually, I"ve made some Oak Leaf wine which is a lovely golden green colour and exactly right for this. We do have a priest and priestess on this occasion, who kneel at the centre touching fingertips over the cauldron which contains roses, and other flowers.

Two people stand at the gate they are the guardians, the woman holding a wooden bowl and the man a bunch of ribbons. A fifth woman has led the rest of the group to the gate, where they stop to be greeted by the guardians and welcomed to the rite of Summer. As they go through the gate they place their fruit in the bowl and are given a ribbon then they go to the circle walking sunwise, deosil, (pronounced jessil). The bowl of fruit is placed with the other offerings in the centre and the priestess goes round the circle collecting the flowers, which are arranged in a large bucket holding water. This is not the place to start singing *"There's a hole in my bucket"*.

The priest is called the Officer of the Sun, who states the intent of the rite.

> *"Good people, this is the longest day of the year and at midday the Lord of the Sun attained His full strength. We are gathered here to celebrate the glory of the Sun in Splendour."*

He continues with a short eulogy, and introduces our old friend, the weaving dance.

While this is happening, the Priestess greets the Earth Mother with words about Her crops and flowers and describes the colour of Her gown, which is, at this time, all shades of green and gold, not to mention the colours of the flowers. She says that we may look for her in the raindrops and the rivers, in the rainbow and the honeysuckle. In the light shining through a park fountain and the light glowing on the moors. She can be seen in everything of beauty on the Earth. When the priestess has finished the dance winds down.

All ask that life may be given and renewed, nurtured and protected. The bowl of fruit is handed round by one of the women in the circle. The honey cakes and wine are blessed, not by sticking the point of a blade into the cup and muttering words about "as the blade is to the cup etc".

Each person is offered a piece of cake which is eaten, except for the small amount crumbled to earth for the small creatures. The cup of golden wine is passed round, always using two hands. Then the rite is ended and the fires and flares put out and we break for a feast. Usually we go somewhere to change our robes and as my garden is fairly big we use this. We have a barbeque, lots of salad and plenty of fruit, not to mention quite a lot of wine.

X   X   X   X

Midsummer

This comes some three days after the solstice. You will remember that I told you that sunrise and sunset remain the same for the day before and the day after solstice-time. Three mornings later, a watcher can actually see that the sun is rising slightly further south and by the same token, the clocks at Greenwich can pick up the change in time. The Greenwich Observatory is no longer in that beautiful building on the Thames but at Cambridge.

The Midsummer Rite

This is a very private affair and takes place at midday. It is a rite for the Land and owes much to Kipling's *"Puck of Pook's Hill."* I choose a secluded place, where Oak, Ash and Thorn grows. If it contains a fairy ring so much the better. This is our natural circle. If there are five of us we stand at 72 degree intervals in the manner of a pentagram, representing Spirit, Air, Fire Water and Earth. If there are fewer, we stand or sit as is possible. In any case we hold small bunches of these leaves and try to recite the piece from the "Dream" concerning the fairies. We do not do it three times and so far we have not heard a voice like "deep as three cows lowing" say "What hempen homespuns have we here?" but we always hope.

This rite is done to Puck, 'The Old One' as Kipling called him. We call upon all who have served the Land to help and protect it throughout the coming year, and then we lie down in the grass of the meadow and meditate on what we particularly wish to put right. We have a little food to share between us and the wild things and a small libation for the Land. When we are ready we give thanks, step carefully out of the circle, leaving our bunches of leaves, and go home. It is a good little rite and nearly always succeeds. I think I said somewhere before that the best things are always the simplest.

X   X   X   X

On Midsummer Day, one should decorate the house with birch twigs and roses. It is considered very unlucky to hear the cuckoo and indeed, she is not supposed to sing on this day.

This seems to be a good time for old saws about the weather. When gnats dance up and down, good weather is on the way; but if they buzz about and sting, there will be prolonged rain.

There is a lovely superstition about butterflies. If the first one you see is white, you will eat white bread for the rest of the year but if it is brown, you will only be able to afford the inferior brown. This was written before we all became so finicky about our diet and we might curl our lip now. But when this belief was in vogue most people could only afford bread made from the sweepings of the mill and that was brown, of course. White bread was a luxury few could afford, so this was a promise of prosperity.

From a gardeners' point of view, white butterflies are a bit of a problem and they eat the cabbages that the cottagers rely upon. In an old cottage garden, where pesticides were not used, they could destroy any crop and would cause destitution.

It was about this time of year that I made up a spell for my own garden. Beans of all kinds are susceptible to black fly which do not like the herb summer savory or those very small marigolds called. I could not find the savory and was walking round my garden muttering.

"Summer, Summer Savory, I need you for my beans.
I plant when Moon is havery, with marigolds between. "

Don't ask what "havery" means. I haven't got a clue. Misty, perhaps? I also do not know why some old garden spells should be in dog Latin.

A very old one, culled from an ancient book whose author I wot not of, goes thusly:

"Under a waning Moon, break a leaf from the tallest weed. Crush it with your teeth and spit the fragments on the earth and say

"Malum Depuo, Hostem Veneno Caedo Caedo. "

Cut the stalk with a silver knife, spread a handful of salt over the hidden root. Then say:-

All the garden bears witness to this and enemies will soon go. "

Now, I have tried this, with couch grass, and nettles, teasles and dock, and it does not work.

A small blessing will help plants to grow, both quickly and well.

"Beans and peas and lettuces, radishes and beet
Rise up soon and make for me a garnish for my meat.
Blessings once and blessings twice do I give to thee
Something given, something gained, Blessed shalt thou be. "

My garden is a muddle of herbs, flowers and vegetables all growing together. They don't seem to like orderly rows and neither do I.

151

"Thyme and sage for sore throats, Rosemary to darken hair,
Bergamot to make a tea, flax for me to wear.
Cecily to sweeten fruit, Lemon balm for cake
Chive to mix with salad and egg
Mint a thirst to slake.
Each one has another use. Each one is a cure.
Some are mixed with others, some are used quite pure.
The monks of old, with loving care grew herbs and gave the poor a
share
And cottage gardens still are found where Nature's medicines
abound."

St. John presides over Midsummer, the only saint strong enough to overcome the wickedness of the old Sun God. Culpeper says that St. John's Wort is a universal cure, which means that it will cure anything. It does have a serious drawback.

"With this wort, Culpeper says, many a cure is done,
Take too much and you could be allergic to the Sun."

Which would follow, would it not?

This is a little general spell for my garden, feel free to use it.

"In my garden I can grow, herbs and worts enough
To ease a pain, to cure an ache, to cure a nasty cough.
I grow them, as my Granny did and for the reason same
That those who come to me for ease are thankful that they came."

152

The three ladies in the Scottish play who chucked such odd things into their cauldron have always been misunderstood. The *"wool of bat"* can be either Hairy Mullein, *Verbascum Lychnitis* used against dysentery or Woolly Faverel *Draba Incana*, used to ease sciatica. The bit about the poor chap on the gallows is Felonwort "Fel" in this case meaning "bitter"or Bittersweet which is either Meadowsweet *"The smelle thereof maketh the hearte merrie"* or Woody Nightshade, the berries of which, being tied round the head are a sure cure for vertigo. *"Gall of Goat"* is Goat's Rue *Galega Officinalis*, good for pestilential distempers. *"Jew's Liver"* equals Jew's Ear, or Cuckoo Pint *Arum Vulgare*, which dried, and pounded is a remedy for poison and the plague. Only use the root though, all the rest of the plant IS poisonous. The poor used to dig up the roots and boil them to add to their meagre diet. *"Eye of Newt"* is Rocket, which is set to become one of the "in" culinary herbs. A stew made from these ingredients might make you sick, but you wouldn't get sciatica, vertigo or the plague.

The Midsummer Tree

This has to be the Oak *Quercus robar*, the Common or Pendulate Oak or *Quercus petraea*, the Sessile or Durmast Oak. Both known to our forbears as *Duir*, which might mean "door' derived from the Sanskrit *"dwr'*. It is called *Darroch* in Gaelic. It is one of the native trees of Britain and it supports a huge variety of both insect and other life. Many different types of moth, for instance and the purple hairstreak butterfly. The number of creepy crawlies living in one tree could fill a book on entomology (which this isn't).

A tree of Lightning, of great age. A tree which has been used to represent all the most enduring qualities of the native people of these islands. "Hearts of Oak," are our seamen, and the "wooden walls" were their ships.

153

The oak is the symbol of the Summer God, who took over the protection of the people from the Holly on May Eve, and to whom He will relinquish it at Samhaine. The other half of the God Looking Both Ways. It is suitable that this month should be dedicated to this mighty tree because at May Eve, the leaves are hardly to be seen. Now we see Him in all His glory, there might still even be red tips to the leaves.

It is a tree of Jupiter and of Hercules, and some believe that the great Cerne Abbas Giant was indeed this huge, thick warrior. It is the Norse god Thor and most of the other thunder gods.

We used to display it on our coins and many families have taken it for their arms, Baldwin and Trelawney in England; Cameron and Buchannan in Scotland. This tree has made a good hiding place for kings and a venerated ground for preachers. King Athelstan refused to meet the Danes within his hall and insisted that the envoys meet him beneath an Oak, he did the same for an embassage from the Pope.

So much has been written about the oak, both from the mythological and the botanical point of view that I really do not find it necessary to repeat it all.

The acorns were said to staunch bleeding, cure the bloody flux, which was dysentery and cure 'drunkenness'. A distillation, called *Spititus Glandium Quercus* was a cure for alcoholism. An infusion of the bark cures internal haemorrhaging and heal damaged tissue in the stomach and intestines. This I read in David Conway's book *"The Magic of Herbs."* The acorns usually ripen in October. It is said that they can be roasted, ground and used as a substitute for coffee. It is not a good one, dandelion root is better.

He also says that oak leaves in the bath are deodourant and relaxing, soothe inflammation and can be trusted as a "toilette de Venus." So there!!!

154

Oak Leaf Wine

I have mentioned this as a possibility for the evening Solstice rite.

You will need:-

4^1/$_2$ Litres (very roughly one gallon) of young oak leaves

The same of water
1 kg or one bag of sugar
3 oranges
Yeast
Pectinol

Pick the leaves when they are very young and fresh, about the last week in May or the first in June. Boil the water and pour onto the leaves, leave overnight. Strain out the leaves and boil the liquid for 20 minutes, then add the sugar, the juice of the oranges and the grated rind.

When the liquor has cooled to blood heat, add the yeast. Leave to ferment in an open bucket for five days and then transfer to a fermentation jar. Fit an airlock and leave to ferment until it stops working and the sediment settles.

At this point rack off into a clean jar, add the pectinol to remove the haze, Leave for 24 hours and filter into sterilised bottles. Boil the corks for ten minutes and then cork the bottles.

This recipe comes from Violet Ricketts. It has been changed slightly to make it dryer. It is a successful recipe and is really quite delicious. Do not allow it to keep. It is much better drunk very young. In fact, if you make it in May you can drink it at that year's solstice.

Midsummer Herb

Balm
Melissa officianalis

As this herb is ruled by Jupiter in Cancer it is appropriate to this time. It is a delicious herb, but does not dry well in home conditions. It spreads like fun and once planted in a garden spreads everywhere.

Melissa is the Latin for Bee, and it is often known as Bee balm. Bee keepers used to rub the leaves round the inside of the hives to promote well-being in their swarms. It was one of the herbs sacred to the temples of Diana.

I have often used the leaves to line a sponge sandwich tin before putting in the batter, it gives a lovely, light lemony fragrance to the cake. Culpeper recommended that a syrup be made to give comfort to stomachs which were out of sorts. It is yet another herb which will cure the bite of a scorpion or that of a mad dog. Considering how feared rabies is, one would think that the whole of Europe would be sown with the plant.

This herb can be used in many homemade cosmetics, giving a fresher scent than roses or lavender. To make a hand lotion mix 5 parts of glycerine to 15 of a prepared Lemon Balm water and a pinch of borax. This is light but keeps the hands in good condition.

It makes a good tonic and restorative for the hair:

Infuse in olive oil: sage, thyme, marjoram and balm. (These are all Live-Forever herbs). Allow to stand for seven or eight days before straining. Rub into scalp before shampooing.

To make an oil for bruises, take balm, rosemary, chamomile flowers, sage, feverfew, lavender tops, southernwood, betony and wormwood a handful of each. Put into a stone jar with enough oil to cover them and stand for a fortnight, stirring often. Boil gently until the oil is extracted, that is until the herbs are crisp but do not exceed the heat of boiling water, which is 120°. Strain through linen and keep in a well corked or screwed bottle. This is a well tried recipe and is very useful for bruises.

To Make a Talisman Against Illness

Work on a Sunday at noon, when the Moon is waxing, as near as possible to the second half of the first quarter. I always find that the day after the quarter is best. Prepare your temple as you would normally do. This means cleaning it, vacuuming and dusting, making sure everything you use is newly cleaned. Make an incense of frankincense, cinnamon, red sandalwood and oak leaves. You can go the whole hog and wear a yellow robe, but try to burn either a gold or yellow candle. Make up a golden silk or velvet pouch.

Talismans usually carry cabbalistic symbols but you can use the birth sign, the name for whom you are doing this, and where she/he was born, plus the sign of the sun and, if you can, the symbol of the planet which governs the afflicted part of the body. Inscribe this on golden paper, don't use metal unless you can afford gold, and this should be pure 24 carat.

Decorate your altar with flowers and herbs of the Sun, St. John's Wort, Rosemary, although this is often dedicated elsewhere,

Mistletoe, Marigold and Celandine, which will probably be over by now. Chamomile and Bay are good herbs, and you can use Lovage. You can find the rulers of these flowers and herbs in Culpeper.

Place your materials on the altar, light the golden candle and say:-

"This candle signifies the light of healing."

Pass your materials through the smoke of the incense and say something about the work you are doing, mentioning the name of the person and the time of the day. Never mind the bit about, "As I will so may it be." It isn't your will that counts. A little humility goes a long way when asking a boon from the Gods. You can meditate, seeing the recipient getting better with the talisman you are making. Inscribe the symbols on the disc. Pass it through the incense again, and over pure water. Put the talisman inside the pouch and once again pass through the smoke. Leave beside the candle until the flame has gone out.

Once again, I'm not sure if this is mine, if not I owe it to Jane Lyle the editor, who added so much to the original book.

Chapter Seven

Lughnasad Lammas

August 2nd

The first day of Autumn. We are celebrating the beginning of the Harvest and mourning the sacrifice of John Barleycorn. The Sun God, Questing Hero has reach the end of His quest and has come to Lughnasad, the Death of Light.

Lammas comes from the word *Hlaf-mass*, meaning the Feast of Bread. Whether this word is Angle or Saxon is irrelevant but all over Europe there were rituals to celebrate the grinding of the first corn and the baking of the first loaf of harvest. The Earth Mother was praised, whatever Her name happened to be.

We do this rite in two parts, but this time one follows the other, with no interval. The first part is done by the men, with the women watching. It tells of the growth of the Sun, from the Winter Solstice to His decline after the Summer festival. How He has given us of His strength and Light and has protected us since May Eve, taking care of the Mother, who bears His child, the Spring.

Now He has reached the end of His quest for the place of sacrifice and will be cut down to feed and nourish His people. Part of Him stays, in His being as the Lord of the Oak, to continue protecting the people until Samhaine.

This is a solemn ritual, reminding everyone that sooner or later, he or she must also be cut down, the only certainty of Life, is Death by the Grim Reaper who if you read Terry Pratchett you will know as someone who speaks only in CAPITALS.

We sing the ancient song of the harvest:-

"John Barleycorn, is cut down dead, it is His time to die
The Sun that warmed our summer days, no longer is so high.
We praise him and our Goddess fair, We thank Him for the corn,
We gather in our harvest now and leave the fields forlorn."

We drink our beer and eat our bread and this part of the rite is closed.

The second part is done in the circle, with everyone present taking part. This is mainly a thanksgiving for the Harvest and a blessing upon the Earth Mother for Her bounty. As we give thanks for the first loaf we look forward to the end of the harvest, when all is safely gathered in to see us through the short days and long, hungry nights of winter.

We look back over the summer which has now passed and hope that the good weather will stay with us until Samhaine, that is throughout the Autumn and the whole time of harvest, because we must remember that it is not just the wheat, barley and oats we think about, but the fruit Cox's Orange Pippins should not be picked until late October. Grapes are picked then; berries and nuts are not ready to be picked until almost the beginning of November.

Within the circle the priestess speaks:

> *"This is the beginning of harvest. At this time, long ago, our ancestors went into the fields to garner the first ripened ears of corn. These were brought back to the tribe with great rejoicing and the women ground the seeds to make the first bread of the season.*

160

This loaf was held to be particularly sacred and the festival of the First Loaf was consecrated. This loaf was shared among the whole tribe and however small the loaf, it would have been taboo for any member to be left out.

Today, we celebrate also and we acknowledge the part played by the Lord in His three aspects.

We remember also our younger brothers in life. They too, are beginning to collect their stores for winter, as the migrants leave us.

*The summer has been cool and wet (*or hot and sunny as the case may be*) yet Our Lady Mother the Earth has given us abundance. The days are getting shorter and we know that when the harvest is completed, Autumn will also be over and then will be the time to gather the last fruit and berries."*

The Priest says:-

"The corn is ripe and the grass is still lush and green. We, the Children of the Goddess, look forward to the harvest. The Great Wheel is turning towards the mists of Autumn and we gather the bountiful fruit of Earth as we begin to gather in ourselves.

We pray for good weather now to gather in the harvest standing in the fields, for soft winds to dry the grain and the straw. Let us give our love and praise to the Lord and Lady who have shown their love for us."

The Priest then invokes the Goddess into the Priestess and says:-

"Hear the words of the Lady."

The Priestess says:-

"My beloved children, listen to the words I whisper in the corn. Watch for my cloak of green moving through the long

161

grass of the meadow like the waves of the sea. My Earth teems with life, food grows in abundance. The young nestlings have long left their nests and many have begun the long journey South. The young animals, born in Spring have come to their strength, already having learned the lessons they will need to survive the winter.

The rivers abound with fish in their prime.

Herbs, fruit and nuts will soon have given of their best, to be gathered in or left to die away in the long sleep of winter.

As the wheel spins, they blossom, seed and die, to be born again. The dying of Summer may make you feel sad but always remember My promise - Spring follows Winter, as Day follows Night, and in order to grow, you must let go, for you cannot stand still while all else moves.

The greenwood is full of birdsong and small creatures are busy about their lives and there, Our Lord Herne awaits His return at Samhaine. The Sun still warms our days and gives us time for the gathering and the nights now are magical with mist.

I am She who Was, Is and Will Be and my love grows with each turn of the Wheel."

There is a moment of stillness and quiet.

The Priestess invokes the Lord into the Priest, who says:-

"Hear My words, good people. My woods are full of melody as the trees sway in the wind and the birds sing. Squirrels have begun their search for nuts; badgers and small creatures play beneath the Harvest Moon. Owls cry in the still, warm night and we hear the first tentative calls of the vixen and the dog fox. Soon the forests will ring to the sound of the rut.

162

Summer nears its end and My days of rest in the Greenwood are nearly over. Soon the Autumn gales will bare the branches of the trees and it will be time for Me to return as Hunter and Protector of My people.

Store up the harvest, draw strength from the Sun and be ready to greet Me at Samhaine."

He then leads everyone round the circle seven times, drawing strength from the Sun and the Earth into Himself and His followers.

There is a sharing of Wine and the First Loaf and the Barley Cake.

Everyone says:-

"We Drink to the Harvest and the abundance of the Earth.

We share the fruits of the Harvest and give thanks to the Mother."

"Let us dwell on the bounty of the Goddess."

Pause

"Let us dwell on the strength of the Lord."

Pause

There are two ways this rite can be ended. Either you simply walk round widdershins three times and close it. Or you can walk round singing the verse of *John Barleycorn* which we sang at the beginning. You will walk round three times and leave the circle, so that, cosmically, your voices fade into the distance, leaving the circle to dissipate.

Old Household Spells

This is a good time to think about the household and there are several old spells for doing just this.

The first is, pluck five shoots from a golden broom bush and using them as tapers, carry them through the rooms, asking for good fortune to smile upon your house, saying

> *Wraithes of the House, take heart and fire.*
> *To every chamber light I give.*
> *To every corner breath I send*
> *To help this house in which I live.*

You can add to the efficacy of this by sprinkling the floor with orris root, tea leaves and salt and then sweeping the floor absolutely clean.

Once fires have to be lit it is as well to remember that fire, though a good and faithful friend if cared for becomes a deadly enemy if allowed to get our of control, so a spell to keep one safe from fire is a good idea but rather like Mrs. Beeton, who began her recipe for jugged hare with the immortal words. *"First catch your hare."* this one presupposes that you keep a fire elemental about your person. i.e. First catch your Salamander. You must catch him in a cage of woven willows and get him home before he burns it, so it needs a fair old turn of speed. Set him down before the fireplace and cross some withies or osiers, (slim willow wands). Set fire to them and put them out quickly with freshly drawn well water. It is as well to have prepared this earlier, don't leave it until the cage is burning merrily or you will lose your house altogether. As you perform this little trick say,

> *"Salamander, Salamander, turn Fire to Water*
> *Under this house and over this house"*

I think this should be done with Undines, but unless you know of an enchanted lake they are difficult to find and even more difficult to catch.

164

The Lammas Tree

The Hazel
Corylus Avellana   Coll

This is the ninth tree
of the old tree alpha-
bet. Each tree had a
meaning and the old
wise ones sent mess-
ages using the leaves
strung on a stick, which
were carried by runners
over long distances. This
might even be the origin of
the *Language of Flowers*,
so beloved of Victorians.

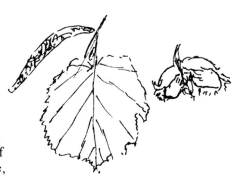

It is not officially a tree but rather a shrub. It can reach a
diameter of over twelve inches in diameter though so it isn't all
that small. It was one of the first trees to colonise the island after
the ice retreated. There is even a possibility that it was here
during the last glaciation, in small, sheltered areas. It never lives
long as it stands, but when it is coppiced, as it usually is, the
stools can be over two thousand years old. It is called *"cailltuin"* in
Scotland and is the badge of the clan Colquhoun, and one of the
names of Scotland, Caledonia came from '*cal dun*' meaning the
hill of the hazel. The very ancient forest of Caledon, in which
Merlin is said to have run mad, covers a large part of the lowlands
and borders.

It was called Coll by the Celts and was a tree of wisdom, but has
been dedicated to Mercury as the God of communication. Connla's
Well, which we find in Irish legend, was the home of the Most
Ancient One, the Salmon, who fed upon the nuts which fell from
the hazels which surrounded it. The spots on its skin were
supposed to be a record of the nuts it had eaten. It was considered

165

to be the wisest of all creatures. Salmon rods were traditionally made from hazel wands, perhaps a remembrance of this legend.

It is probably the favourite tree of the water diviner, and the ancient Druids used hazel rods to find hidden wells or hidden sources of water. This is actually, the only wand you need. I know it is fashionable to have a different one for every day, but one is all you need. Silver, black coral, even lignum vitae makes no difference. A hazel wand will point just as well as anything else and it does have a real pedigree. It was also used to find thieves and murderers.

If you wished to be invisible in the Middle Ages, which was on the whole quite a good time to be able to do this, you could carry a hazel twig and eat fern seed. This alone was supposed to have this ability, but you had to gather it under very special circumstances.

The nut, like the hard-boiled egg, is one of the original pre-packed lunches. They are easy to carry and will keep you going for a long time. They are full of vitamins and real goodness. They are a wonderful protein substitute. Weight for weight they contain fifty per cent more protein, seven times more fat and five times more carbohydrate than hen's eggs. This from Richard Mabey's good book *"Food for Free"*. He also gives a fifteenth century recipe which sounds marvellous and has Gyngere and Safroun in its ingredients.

According to Culpeper the milk, mixed with honey and water is good for an old cough. And the dried husks and shells or the skins of the nut, to the weight of two drams, taken in red wine can stay a haemorrhage. They are also good for the heart.

Mixed with purslane, jasmine, periwinkle and an anemone they were rumoured to be an aphrodisiac.

A double hazel nut, carried in the pocket was a sure cure for tooth-ache.

But not all the portents were good ones, *"The more hazelnuts, the more bastards."* was a belief in the Midlands, perhaps "Nutting" and all that protein were responsible. I remember going out 'nutting' with my whole family when I was very young and before the First War, village schools closed on Holy Cross Day, which was September 14th to allow the children to spend the day harvesting what nuts the squirrels had left.

Oh, if the shells were thick the winter would be bleak, with deep snow and low temperatures, gales and iron-hard ice.

The Lammas Plant

Barley
Hordeum vulgare

This is a plant which belongs particularly to this time. Virgo is a sign of Earth and this is the sheaf carried by most of the Earth Goddesses. A corn dolly, traditionally made from barley straw, would be hung in the house to attract health and wealth.

It reminds us of the Cult of Barley, when Cronos, that is Time, was sacrificed with a sickle and his blood spilt upon the ground to bring fertility to the Earth. He, having been castrated, was no longer fertile, and so had to be killed. This is our own John Barleycorn.

The barley cakes we eat should be crossed with an eight pointed cross, a symbol of the Sun. The sun cults did not set much store by the number seven, which was sacred to the Moon. Eight was their number, which is a number multiplied by itself 2x2=4 x2=8. Some ancient warriors carried sickles into battle with which to castrate their prisoners.

Demeter, the old Corn Goddess, mother of Persephone, sent her favourite Triptolemus carrying a bag of barley seed, down to the world of men to teach them about agriculture. When they managed to grow fertile seed they turned from being hunter-gatherers to being farmers.

If you make barley water to quench your thirst, you can use the barley again in love spells and to cure toothache in the sympathetic way. Wrap a barley straw round a stone and throw the stone into a river. Visualise the water washing the pain away and say

"As I throw thee, water take thee, away, away."

The Lammas Flower

Poppy
Papaver

There are so many varieties of these, from black, field, red, not to mention opium, (I told you not to mention it).

It was the blood of the aforementioned God, Cronos. It also represents the blood spilt in many wars as we know from Flanders and the British Legion ceremony in November.

It is a very effective nerve tonic. It can be used to attract money. Gild the heads and use then as a decoration in the home.

There is a spell for a questioner. Write your question in blue ink on white paper and put it into a poppy seed pod. Put this under your pillow. This is no time to pretend you are a princess with a pea. The answer to your question should come into your dreams. The spell is:

"A seed case full of wisdom and grace,
Inside your head my question I place,
Beneath my pillow through the night
And I shall dream the answer right."

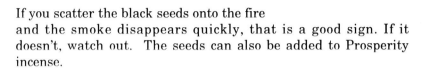

If you wish to become pregnant you could
add the seeds to your food.

If you scatter the black seeds onto the fire
and the smoke disappears quickly, that is a good sign. If it
doesn't, watch out. The seeds can also be added to Prosperity
incense.

Lammas is in Leo, of course, not Virgo, but
the harvest carries on through that sign and
Libra and even a little bit of Scorpio. Leo
rules the heart and is associated with
success. As the harvest has just begun this
is no bad thing. The colour is greenish
yellow, the colour of the corn just before it
ripens.

The metal is gold as Leo is ruled by the Sun,
but once again the harvest comes in Virgo,
ruled by Mercury and Libra ruled by Venus,
but we will speak more about Venus in the
next chapter.

Gold is the purest metal which does not tarnish. I read
somewhere that all the plates and cooking utensils in Atlantis
were made of gold. The only thing guaranteed to tarnish it is the
greed of the men who mine it or possibly not them but the owners
of the mines. I think about the Gold rush into the sacred Black
Hills of the Sioux and the way those natives were treated. Only
now, large parts of the rainforest are being destroyed by men
rushing into a restricted area because gold has been found there.

We very rarely have pure gold, though do we? We have nine carat,
and fourteen carat, both impure and mixed with baser metals. I

169

lived in the East for several years and the merchants in the gold souks of Baghdad would never have tolerated anything but twenty-four carat, almost as pure as you can get.

There seems to be such a difference of opinion about the jewel, I have found, red Carnelian, Zircon, Tiger's Eye, Red Banded Agate, (this is Graves) and even Amethyst. As I am not an expert on gemstones it is best that you make up your own mind.

A Chant for a Journey

It is a good idea to have a spell that you can mutter under your breath as you begin a journey. I have one which I address to the "Great God of Going" my friend Herme again, who is Old Mercury the God of Travellers. If I forget to do this before I start, I have to stop the car halfway down the hill, get out and say it or I am not comfortable. It follows that when you come home safely you thank the same beings. I do not give away my own charm, but here is one I made earlier.

> "The journey I make is one of need,
> I ask the God to pay me heed
> That I may safely homeward come,
> There and back when my work is done.

May the God of Going hear my call
On my going and coming no ill befall.
May I drive with care and may those I meet
Be safe and careful on the street."

It might be a good idea if you did this the first time within the house, before you set out, using yellow candles and the incense of Mercury. The one I use is based on the Leo Vinci book *"Incense - It's Ritual Significance, Use and Preparation."* He gives two, the one I like best is composed of Cinnamon, Herb Mercury, Marjoram, Lime flowers, and Lemon Peel. I try not to use imported and expensive gums, so I use Plum gum, picked from plum trees in March, when there is usually rather a lot of it; as he uses Larch, I use Larch gum, collected the same way, and Hazel catkins, which he doesn't use at all, but I find very good. You can also add a few Larch needles. This is the only conifer which sheds them in winter. You can also make yourself a little sachet filled with dried comfrey. This is a herb particularly suited to this work.

The Tarot card is Strength, Tath number eight and it has an affinity with eating, suitable for the harvest. It symbolises the ancient Serpent power, which I find strange in anything as masculine as Leo. The Serpent was Tiamat, the early Chaldean goddess Creation, who was associated with Nuit, the Egyptian goddess of the Stars, seen in her glory in the Milky Way. I always think of the Serpent or Dragon Power as being feminine, not logical or calculating but untamed, chaotic force.

Chapter Eight

Alban Elfed

The Autumnal Equinox

This is the balance of the second half of the solar year. Most of the harvest has been brought home and with the mists of Autumn comes the time to say goodbye to the strength of the Sun, unless we are lucky enough to have a St Luke's summer.

It is a time of wonder as we watch the changing colours of the trees and time to gather up the fallen little green crab apples which make such a delicious jelly to eat with our lamb and pork. There are rowan berries for beef and quince for the rare occasions when we can afford pheasant or venison.

We gather elderberries to make Elder Rob, to soothe coughs and colds and give us just about the best vitamin C we can find. Once the first frosts come we can pick the sloes for the sloe gin which keeps us so warm in winter.

We pick and dry hawthorn berries for the birds and keep some back to make a strong potion for high blood pressure, and we watch the sunflowers to gather the ripened seed, also for the birds, although many people add them to bread and scones now.

Teasels both for brushing woolies to take away those annoying bobbles; and kex, which is the stalk of hedge parsley and a wonderful word to remember for long winter evenings playing scrabble. Both of these can be sprayed to make decorations for later in the year.

172

One of the prettiest berries is that of the spindle. If you see this little shrub in a hedgerow it means that it is at least five hundred years old. The flesh of the berry is pink but the large seeds are bright orange, the small spear shaped leaves show some lovely colours. It was used to make meat skewers, because it does not splinter. It is a pity that so few of our trees turn scarlet in the Autumn. Only maple does this. Even our native field maple goes red sometimes. Elder can be a pretty shade of pink, and both hawthorn and the wayfaring tree show deep reds and purples.

When we do this rite we ask everyone to bring a candle in a jar, the top tied round with a loop of string, which makes it much easier to carry. This should be at least a third filled with sand or earth but the candle probably won't stay upright unless you make a hole in the centre and fill it with melted wax.

They should also bring something symbolic of the harvest, a piece of local fruit and a few ears of corn, that means wheat or barley in Britain not maize; and one or two of the following: sprigs from an oak tree, some pine cones and some autumn flowers. We stipulate that these things must be gathered from their homes and brought with them, not picked as they go down to do the rite. We do not want the trees and bushes around the house stripped because people are too lazy to go out and do their own hunting. These things are to be each person's gift to the Gods.

An altar, made from large flat stones or a fallen log has been found upon which stands a bowl of clear spring water, symbolic of the Mother. This is surrounded by berries and fruit. A fire has been lit outside the circle in the South, to symbolise the sun which is leaving us.

We have the usual quarters, and at one point each person walks round the circle and casts his offering into the fire as a token of his thanks to the Sun for his blessings throughout the summer. This is NOT a 'give-away' so do not make it negative.

Then we form two circles, women inside men out. The men as usual, go sunwise and the women widdershins, no weaving, just a straight circle and as we go we chant:

"The wheel turns on to Autumn time
The Gods are strong and in their
prime.

We give our love and thanks anew
Oh. God and Goddess, praise to you.
O Power bring the balance in
As the Wheel retains it's spin.

There is more, but this is a spell we
have performed and the power must
not be dissipated. When it is finished,
we stretch out our arms, visualising
balance and power.

This should be held until the priestess says that the thing is done
and so it will be. We share cakes and wine, dark red in this case,
and the rite is closed.

Now the next bit seems to be a game, and at first, some of the
group, especially those who were new to us really only wanted to
stand about in their pretty frocks and be intoned over. That is
what they considered a "real rite" to be. We pointed out that this
"Game" was far more authentic than any of the standing about
ones, with priests and priestesses invoking Gods and Goddesses
who were probably too busy elsewhere anyway.

This is a traditional and actual harvest game and it was prepared
by Steve Morris, who has kindly allowed me to include it here.

We try to get equal numbers of men and
women or children, for they do enjoy taking
part in this. One of my grand-daughters
usually has to be the token female in the
men's party, because where her big brother
goes, she goes too or the hills are not alive
with the sound of music but a red-faced and
hugely annoyed little girl voicing her
indignation very loudly indeed.

174

I do ask people to wear old clothes, and leave a change of raiment back at the ranch. These are essential as is the towel I ask them to bring. A lot of moisture is displaced.

We find a place for "Home" where there is a low wall or a very large rock. A sheaf of wheat, barley and oats tied with a red ribbon has been placed out of sight and hearing. The "table' ideally should be sited so that it can be approached from any one of several directions under cover.

The men go off to "kill" the Bright Lord, represented by the sheaf. They carry with them copious amounts of ale, and a sickle. This is a very old one, found in one of my outhouses as they were being demolished and it has a nasty habit of coming apart as it is being thrown leaving the thrower with the handle and the blade curving through the air, to the frightened wails of the spectators. No-one has yet thought of mending it and anyway, what's a nasty cut with a rusty sickle between friends?

The women are busy preparing the table, which represents the cave of the Goddess to which the slain Hero is brought.

They set out a feast and prepare devious deterrents for the "invading' men. These were specifically pails of milk and water, but, being devious, crazy foam, green slime and soot are added. This is a secret and the men don't know it yet. They also do not know where "home" is, part of the game is finding it. So it is not prepared until they have gone.

They set up the sheaf in their prepared place and sing songs about how brave their are, going off to Kill the Hero in the butchest voices they can manage. They then form a ring round the sheaf, four paces from the centre, one pace for each month of winter and one for luck. The jug is passed round and each man must drink before taking a shy at the sheaf. As you can see, a dodgy sickle should cause some merriment at least. As each one throws, he must say something about the God he hopes to slay. This should go on for some time with much quaffing of ale, until someone knocks or cuts the sheaf down.

After finishing off the ale, they set off to find and attack "home", coming from as many directions as possible, silently at first, then with wild cries as they near their objective.

The women, meanwhile, have been preparing such booby traps as they can devise and filling the buckets, and anything else handy with as much gunk as possible. Soot and water makes a lovely mess, especially if a little milk is added. Crazy foam on paper plates is a good missile. You can see the need for a change of clothes.

Once the men have launched their attack it is essential that they be made as wet as possible, especially the one carrying the sheaf, who will be the one who finally cuts it. This usually ends with a frontal attack with the men passing the sheaf like a rugby ball, most of ours have played this game at some time. A constant rain of messy water and foam-filled plates meets this attack, and anyone silly enough to fall down is plastered. Everyone gets delightfully messy, because of course, the men manage to get some of the water containers and the plates.

This is acting out a fertility rite. The man who places the sheaf on the table and the woman who got in the first good shot with water become the priest and priestess.

We gather round the table and the women sing;

> "Let us welcome home the fallen
> To the Goddess all return,
> The seed shall fertilise the womb
> So that life shall be re-born."

The sheaf is doused with clean water and it is hung from a branch and the men sing John Barleycorn. The priest and priestess bless the food and ale and are the first to eat and drink, giving what thanks they think fit. Then everything is passed round and we get down to some serious feasting.

176

This festival has its serious side. It is one of balance and points out the need for balance in the relationship of the two sexes, their dependence upon one another and their dependence on the Earth. After the feast, the sheaf is taken down and buried, or kept until spring when part of the Imbolc rite should be the ritual burial of the sheaf. Or it can be placed on the fire. Either way, it must return to earth.

X   X   X   X

The Crab Apple Tree
Malus sylvestris Quert Aball

Again, one of our native trees, and one of the chieftain trees of the Battle. I know that according to all the pundits this month is not equated to the apple tree. Where I come from it most certainly is.

The middle of the apple harvest, which begins in August with Beauty of Bath and ends in November with the gathering of crab apples, Bramleys and Coxs' Orange Pippins. It always makes me hot under the collar when I see English Coxs' on sale in August. When I think of the trouble we used to take to pick 'em just right, that is when the seeds rattle inside, I get quite cross.

The Crab is only a small tree and usually grows singly, in hedgerows and small breaks on a hillside. They seem to like old charcoal burning pits. The fruit is quite small, very rarely more than an inch in diameter and greenish yellow.

Nearly always it has to be picked up from the lane, because the trees are quite tall and no one wants to take a ladder for miles across countryside. They are well worth the trouble though. The jelly made from the juice is fabulous, and seasoned with sage for pork; mint for lamb, and marjoram for anything is one of the best accompaniments to be found. It is not a good idea to eat the things raw, though, they will curdle your gums.

The wood is good for very delicate woodworking, if dried slowly and is sought after by carvers. It was used to make set squares and drawing instruments. All the eating apples we have now come from the crab, which name comes from the adjective 'crabby' meaning awkward, or a tree that bears the wrong fruit, that is very sour.

As this is the season of "mellow fruitfulness" it is a good time to do some spells which involve apples. One of these was written for me especially for the television programme "Earth Magic". It involves a certain amount of hocus-pocus.

"Apple, apple, red as blood
As two become two hearts in one.

(here one cuts the apple in half)

Each one bears the sacred star.

(Apples have a star-shaped calyx)

I call to each one from afar.

A Herb for Her, a Herb for Him

(make a cut in the flesh and insert a piece of Rosemary)

178

A touch of fire to seal it in.

(This is done with a taper lit at a candle. It should make a lovely hissing sound.)

Bind with the cord to make them one.

(tie round with a scarlet cord.)

As I will so be it done."

Go outside and bury the apple in the ground.

I do not recommend anyone doing this spell. I was asked to do it so many times after the programme that it became known as "That dratted apple spell." It was only meant to be an example of how a spell is constructed but the Director was insistent that I tell for whom I had made it. I even invented an imaginary couple who needed help, although throughout my bit of the programme I had insisted that I do not interfere with other people's lives.

The spell was taken extremely seriously by the press, who even wanted to know the outcome and I received many requests to do it for lovelorn members of the public. This was not an old spell culled from an ancient tome found in an attic, written in spidery writing on parchment, the old ink, made from roasted acorns now fading away. It was written by a friend just before the shot was taken but I have been so rude about the bally thing that no good could come of anyone using it. Although, I have to say, that many people over the years have told me that they have used it and it has worked "like a charm".

A real old charm begins: "Pick your apple when the moon has waned three nights, breathe upon it's cheek; rub it with a scarlet cloth and say:

"Fire sweet and fire red, Warm the heart and turn the head."

Kiss the red half, put it into another's hand.

Who holds it shall weaken,
Who eats it shall be yours."

And another

"A bloom on the tree when the apple is ripe
Means a sure termination of somebody's life"

To fall asleep under an apple tree is a good way to be carried off by the fairies and the Apple Tree Man lives in the oldest tree in the orchard. He is always left the last apple of the crop, to ensure that the other trees will bear well the following year.

There is another belief which I have only recently come across. Probably at Samhaine, or possibly at Harvest festival suppers, every person in the room has an apple tied with string which is suspended over a fire. The first one to drop indicates the first person to marry. If your apple doesn't fall, you will stay single.

To test the faithfulness of your lover, drop an apple pip in the fire, saying his name as you do so. If it explodes he is faithful, if it burns away without a sound, he isn't.

I have always liked the idea of the Celtic heaven. A place where the hills are clad with apple trees bearing both blossom and fruit, sure that is where the above superstition of the lone blossom among the fruit comes from.

At one time, anyone who felled an apple tree without very good reason incurred the death penalty. Later on this was commuted to a fine of one cow per tree.

180

It was part of the Great Tree of Munga, a combination of Oak, Hazel and Apple. The name of Apollo probably comes from the same root. This tree produced acorns, hazelnuts and apples at the same time. It was a sanctuary tree and was the shelter of the White Hind, that is the Goddess in the fabled thicket. In Genesis it is the Tree of Knowledge of Good and Evil. The Silver Branch of Celtic mythology was cut from an apple tree, assumed to be one of those growing in Avalon, the Isle of Apples, to which Arthur was taken after the Battle of Camlann. Nemesis is portrayed carrying an apple branch and the Diana-Nemerensis cult was associated with both the apple and the deer.

The fabled Unicorn rested beneath the apple tree. This gives an equation of Immortality through wisdom. Only a virgin can approach the unicorn, but this is not a girl with an intact hymen but one who retains spiritual integrity. Again, this is the Goddess, who was not a virgin in the Greek sense. This is not to be confused with the Biblical sense. The Hebraic word for virgin actually had two meanings, the first, a young girl with her hymen still intact and the second meaning being a young woman who has not yet born a child. There is a difference.

Graves makes the Vine the tree for this time, but with the apple I prefer the Hop *Humulus lupulus*, which also climbs to a good height. The leaves resemble those of a vine but they are rough

and hairy and can scratch. Like the vine, it makes a wonderful drink. Beer is a good potion at this time of the year. Drying hops are the most soporific scent there is. Going home in September was like stepping into a warm bed. As you stepped off the train a great yawn escaped you and there were no late nights for a week.

Hops are added to most herbal sleep drinks and all the tablets bought in chemists as sleep inducers. It can also do wonders for a vagrant appetite.

Culpeper says that a decoction of the tops cleanses the blood curing things like scurvy, ringworm, the morphew and all discolourings of the skin.

He also says that the young shoots, which appear in March and April, being mild, and served like asparagus, are a very wholesome and pleasant tasting spring food. I spent almost every Easter holiday from school, stooping in cold mud, training the brutes. I never felt like eating them, just as I spent a lot of the summer holidays picking the hops themselves, when I wasn't picking apples. They are very pretty though.

Herb

Yarrow
Achillaea millefolium

This is a plant of the hedgerows, growing in small groups or by itself. It also grows along fences where hedgerows have been. The many little flowers can be creamy white or pinkish. According to Culpeper it is under the governance of Venus, who ruled this time, but from the book of the 11th century Apuleius, comes the tale that "*Achilles, the chieftain found it and he, with this wort healed the them that with iron were stricken and wounded. He healed a man named Telephos.*"

It can be used for toothache, for swellings, for problems of the bladder and this one *"If a man's head burst or a strange swelling appear on it, let him take the roots of this same wort and bind them on his neck; that will be of good service to him."*

"For aches of the bowels and inwards and the hardening of vanes(no not a misprint, that is how it is spelled). If a man drinketh, then it is good for him for whatsoever annoyances he hath within."

According to David Conway in *"The Magic of Herbs"* - *"Yarrow is one of the Witch herbs and carrying it at weddings guaranteed seven years of married bliss."* he adds in brackets (*Then the seven year itch presumably set in.*)

A Kentish rhyme goes:-

"Yarrow, yarrow, the first I've found
In the name of the Lord I pluck thee from the ground.
As the Lord loves the Lady, so warm and so dear
So in my dream may my lover appear."

The festival of the Equinox comes on the cusp of Virgo-Libra, and it is another of the yellow-green colours. It is ruled by Mercury and according to Case it is dominated by the self-conscious initiative, whatever that means.

It is one's own harvest or that which one has acquired for oneself. The Tarot card is the Hermit and the gem the lime green peridot, which just happens to be my favourite stone. It is the only stone I buy and I like it much better than any of the others named for

183

Libra, although if I was in the millionaire class I might like emeralds.

Jacquie Brennan says that it was used to treat the liver and the adrenals, to free the mind from envy and to create emotional stability. Rudolf Steiner says that it activates physical and spiritual sight.

Weather

21st Matthew's day, bright and clear brings good wine in the next year.

A south wind on September 21st indicates that the rest of the Autumn will be warm.

20th, 21st and 22nd These three days rule the weather for October, November and December.

Shut up your bees on the equinox.

And St Matthew's rain fattens pigs and geese.

Chapter Nine

Michaelmas
End of the Earth Cycle

I had always wanted to do a rite at this time. The old legend of George killing the Dragon had been grafted onto the even older one of Michael, the great Prince of Light, taming the Dragon of Untamed Force which is usually that of the female. It is near the end of the harvest and time to tidy up before the end of autumn.

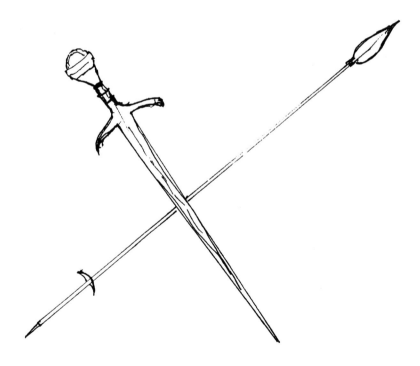

The hills of Michael, usually crowned with the ruins of a church no-one could build are always high and conical and must have been sacred to our forefathers before they were taken over by the Church. Burrowbridge, Brent Tor in Devon, St Michael's Mount in Cornwall and of course, Glastonbury Tor are but a few. They are all on major ley lines and indeed, the great Dragon line, which runs across Southern England from Cornwall to Norfolk begins at St Michael's Mount. These invisible currents of energy link places of great sacredness all over the world.

The Bible says that Michael the great Archangel was given power over the heavens and he is equated with the Primeval Eros, who created the firmament. Michael does not, in fact, slay the Dragon but comes to terms with Her. She represents the Milky Way and raw energy, like Fire in its primal unharnessed form. Michael represents structure which brings the random, chaotic energy to order,

With this in mind, we begin our rite by building as big a cairn as we can find rocks for and we build it round a length of pipe. We do this by the spring site above the great Mayday oak. A fire pit is made at the bottom of the cairn and one to the South, well away from the cairn.

The spring is to the West and there is a great hill to the North, pointed of course, but without a ruined building crowning it. We are open to the East so we have all the elements in the right places. We make a seven ringed spiral from the bottom of the cairn, the outside ring has a diameter of forty-nine feet. This is seven times seven, September used to be the seventh month.

St. Michael's Rite

We gather, in ordinary, clean clothes, as the sun goes down, outside the spiral. Several selected people will have gone into the trees to wait until they are called. Everyone has a candle in a holder, which is unlit. We form into a circle and there is a short opening to the Lord and the Lady. The chosen Michael leads us round the circle and then into the maze-spiral. As the spiral tightens, try to imagine that you are travelling back into your own past. By the time the maze is completed you should be back to the dawn of human history, when the race was without fire, the unlit fire and candles signify this.

We end in a nine foot circle round the cairn, which Michael approaches by himself. He says:-

> "From rock comes iron. From our Stone Age we passed to the Iron Age. The Sword IS in the Stone."

He lights the small fire at the South base of the cairn and at the same time the fire in the South outside the circle is also lit. When they are blazing satisfactorily, he paces round to the North side of the cairn and removes the Sword from the pipe. He carries it back to the South. He passes the blade through the flames and calls out:-

> "The man kind has been without fire. I have brought you this gift. I have purified the blade in the sacred flame. Come to the Fire, each in turn and receive Light."

He lights a branch or taper and each person brings their candle to be lit. When we are back in our circle, we all say:-

"We give thanks for the gift of Fire. May we always use it aright."

Michael then leads the circle outwards, but not unwinding the spiral. As we stand in the outside circle a great roar is heard from the trees. The Dragon of Untamed Force strides out and engages Michael in a stylised physical battle. When they realise that they are evenly matched, they stop. Michael says:-

"The Dragon has been tamed."

The Dragon says:-

"Long have I been ruled by Chaos. Henceforward, I will be the Silver Dragon of Albion, I will give heat and light to those who ask and I will lend my strength to the service of the Light and of the Land, so long as this be needed."

All say:-

"Be it so. We give thanks to our Silver Dragon."

We close to the cairn again and sit in the circle while the story of our search for the Dragon is told.

The Quest for the Dragon

Close your eyes and allow the mists to form around you. Go back through time. You wait for the mist to change from white to orange, dissolving as it does so.

You stand looking into a fire burning in a brazier. You are under the stars in a clearing in the woods Behind you, a hermit's hut offers a little shelter and before you the forest seems alive with half-heard sounds. You are alone, save for your horse which is tethered off to the left. As you wait a feeling of anticipation comes over you and you wish that the light armour you wear was somewhat more substantial. Your sword trembles in your hand as

the feeling grows that something is going to happen. A light is approaching from the opposite side of the clearing and as it gets to the edge, you are only aware of this light. As you watch, it parts and gives the impression of a doorway into the trees.

This is the invitation for which you came and it is your only opportunity to turn back. You hesitate. Do you really want to face what lies ahead?

An ember cracks in the brazier and the spell cast over you loses it's hold for a moment. This is what you came for, after all. You move toward the door and pass from the land you know into the realms that few people know at all and no mortal knows well. You are escorted by many tiny lights showing the way you must take. Behind you the lights go out, and the forest closes in. You do not look back.

The path winds back and forth, first to the left and then to the right. It is not long before you have lost your sense of direction. All you can do is walk the path defined by the lights.

Now the forest is gone and you are on a plain looking out across a sea of mist to an island far off in the morning light. Your escort of lights has gone but you can see well enough. A boat is coming towards you through the mist. Nothing else moves.

There is a figure in the bow of the boat which defies description. It is vaguely human in shape but whether it is male of female, you cannot make out. Even as you step on board the figure remains vague. You speak a greeting but the gentle motion of the boat sliding through the water is your only reply. Time ceases to have any meaning as you glide over the sea through the mist.

The shadow of the boat grows. The mists part and you are ashore.

You have arrived at the Isle of the Dragon. There is no way back.

The land before you slopes up gradually from the shore and then steepens to form a single hill, which is the only way on. Follow the path of scaly stones that leads off up the hill. You expect that it will simply ascend but it turns back on itself, dropping some distance down the hill before another turn finds you climbing again.

The path goes on and on, climbing, dropping, turning and then climbing again. You are beginning to tire and eventually the thought comes to you that you will abandon this quest and try to get back to the safety of your own land. But you force your weary legs onward. Your fatigue and the desire to turn back becomes so strong that you wonder if it is only your body making you feel this way.

At last you stop.

You look round you and see that you are still on the same path but for all your effort you are only about two hundred yards from where you first stepped ashore. Going on from here is one of the hardest things you have ever done. The ache in your legs is intense. The sword you carry has become such a burden that you think seriously about leaving it behind. Worse, you long for the safety of your past and the mounting unease about your future is sapping what is left of your strength.

You force yourself to go on.

The path seems to be a little easier now. It climbs more but twists less however any gratitude you might feel is drowned in the growing fear. You can see nothing but the scaly backbone of the hill you are climbing. No birds sing. There is no sound but the laboured beating of your heart and your gasping breath. Yet you know that soon it will come, whatever the end of you quest might be. You are almost on your knees. Your blood chills from a sudden icy breeze which freezes the sweat on your body. You cannot go on. But you do, dragging the sword behind you now.

The mist returns. You can see nothing. The path ends abruptly and directly in front of you is a pit and you only just manage to prevent yourself from falling in. You send up a rueful little prayer that you were too tired to run for it is not pleasant, this pit. You can see neither the bottom nor the other side. Forcing yourself to stand, you wait. And you do not have to wait long.

A red glow begins to rise from the bottom of the pit and your sweat dries as the chill wind loses its power. Then the temperature begins to rise and the glow in the pit becomes intense. You begin to sweat again. You must run, but where to? You must get away from this accursed place but your feet are rooted to the spot. The ground is beginning to vibrate and the air is scorching. You can feel the sword in your hand burning your skin. You will be consumed in this unbearable heat. Your thin armour is now burning metal and you begin to panic. A voice in your head screams at you to throw the sword away, tear the armour off before you are burned to the bone.

Then, the very last remnants of your warrior's pride prevents you from casting away your only means of defence. Instead, you raise the sword over your head in the St. George's parry as the blinding light finally emerges from the pit. The Earth itself crashes too as the Dragon emerges from its lair. The pit has gone and there is nothing but the sword in your hand and the dazzling radiance of the ageless Dragon.

You know that you cannot win but you must try. With all the concentrated effort of your mind dedicated to a single stroke, you match the chaotic power of the beast, and as your sword strikes,

191

power and will touch and mingle. The heat goes and a cool breath of understanding comes from the Silver Dragon of Albion.

Darkness.

The peace of oblivion passes and you regain your identity. At last you know. You ARE Michael AND you are the Dragon. As you contemplate your new state of being you find that your body has been consumed in defeating the beast. Yet you are not formless. Men have raised a memorial to you. A stone tower to last forever. On hills all over the land they have raised towers to commemmorate your act of mediating the blind energy of the stars. They do not realise that the contest was drawn, not won. Man sees himself as the master of energy but you know differently.

You can only watch as man's arrogance and selfseeking abuses the power you won for him at such cost. In the face of this ignorance and greed, how much longer will the Great Dragon be prepared to stay down? Would you be prepared to fight once again for the race man has become?

We are all St. Michael and we are all the Dragon and we are equally, the race of the man kind. Remember this, as the mists swirl about you and your return and remember.

Silence for a short time.

Then Michael leads us back unravelling the maze. The Silver Dragon brings up the rear. As we go, each one brings himself back to the now, as we walk through the spiral of time to the present. At the wide outside circle again we turn once more to face the cairn. A cup and oatcakes are passed round.

We close with thanks to the fire. Praise to the Light and the Land, now with the power of both Michael and the Silver Dragon. We say Hail and Farewell to the Lord and Lady. There is a blessing. And the Rite is ended.

X   X   X   X

Michael only comes to terms with the Dragon. Unlike St. George, he does not defeat or kill her. If you can get hold of it, there is a wonderful book by Kenneth Grahame called *"The Reluctant Dragon."* It is a children's book but quite easy for grown-ups to read. Apart from the beautiful English it puts even the rather arrogant George in perspective.

The Dragon symbolises raw energy, the element of fire in its unharnessed sense. Michael is therefore the representative of that which brings the random, chaotic energy into harness. Depending on your view of chaos, he is either the conquering hero or the villain of the piece. Because he represents the emblem of progress and control, which is essentially male, he is thought to ignore the natural and splendid laws of entropy, which are essentially female. He, like the male dominated governments of our planet have decided that the universe is a better place if it passes into a totally structured state.

This is still the time when we think of a balance being achieved between night and day, chaos and order, and it is right that it should come in the Sign of Libra. Michael was given power over the heavens, *"Thou too, Michael, who holdest the Heavens."* In miscellaneous Coptic texts, Budge says, *"that when Christ wished to come down to Earth, God called to Him a mighty power in the Heavens that was called Michael, and committed the Christ to its care. The Power descended and was called Mary."* So Michael has impeccable references as a defender.

X   X   X   X   X

Many ancient fairs happened at Michaelmas. The "Statutes" at Burton-on-Trent and the Nottingham Goose Fair are but two. Because Michaelmas is a quarter day, the Hiring fairs all over the country were on this day. Workers looking for new jobs would stand around in a conspicuous place carrying the tools of their trades and wearing a peacock feather in their hats to show that they were for hire. As soon as hands had been slapped, meaning a bargain had been struck, they would remove the feathers and wrap them up carefully until the next year. Hiring was for a year and a day. This could be extended if both parties were agreeable.

A Ghost Story

This is a story I was told when I was a child. It concerns Canterbury Cathedral, which for those of you who do not know, is in Kent.

In the very early Middle Ages, the abbot had a mistress whose name was Nan Cook. Nan the cook she would have been. The abbot began to treat her badly and when she objected, threatened to have her burned as a heretic. She got in first and put powdered glass into his supper. This, not unnaturally, caused him to die in considerable pain. Nan was arrested, tried and was sentenced to death. She had hoped to be hanged, which was a much quicker death than burning and did not carry the months of torture which a trial of heresy carried.

But the monks were not merciful. They dragged her along a very dark passage, which runs between the abbey and the cathedral (the remains of the abbey are now part of King's School) and they walled her up on the 29th September. Since then, her ghost, and those of the monks who did this horrible thing, walk the Dark Entry at 8 o'clock on the evening of Michaelmas.

The Entry used to be locked at each end from about sunset, because it was believed that anyone who saw her and caught her breath, would die before the year was out. In the thirties, two boys from the school hid themselves in the entry. They were frantic when the gates were unlocked, because they had seen the wraith. They were both dead before the end of the year.

Blackberry
Rubus fruticosus

Any animal born at this time of the year was thought to be particularly naughty, and kittens were called Blackberry kittens, because the Devil is supposed to breath on blackberries on

Michaelmas midnight, and this causes the wickedness. If they were tortoise-shell they were supposed to be very lucky, despite their waywardness.

Blackberries are not supposed to be eaten after the 30th. because of this association with the Devil.

He was pushed out of Heaven by Michael on this day and fell into a bramble bush. Therefore he cursed, spat upon, stamped on or trailed his cloak over any brambles left on the bush. You must remember the change of the calender, however. In many places the fruit is not ready to eat until the second week in October.

How true this superstition is, I am not sure. Only once have I put it to the test. One year, I picked a lovely, juicy looking berry, which was occupied by a wasp. I am allergic to wasp stings and spent several days in intensive care and a few more in hospital.

Brambles themselves have been used in many an old cure and were often used for sick animals. Boils, rickets and whooping cough are only some of the illnesses which can be cured by crawling through a bramble bush. Burns were treated with bramble leaves while chanting the following sloka, "which as you have not heard I will proceed to relate".

> "There came three angels out of the East
> One brought Fire and two brought Frost
> Out Fire, In Frost."

Later Christianity added "In the name of the Father, son and Holy Ghost" replacing the trinity of the Goddess.

The plant is attributed to Venus, by Culpeper, but now it is mostly to Bridget, her ancient name being Bride the Maiden Goddess.

It was sacred to many pagan deities and much used in worship. It was used in charms and spells and in sachets for healing, money and protection. Any blackberry bush which forms a natural arch is used in magical healing, as I have already quoted. What I did not say was that you crawled through the bush backwards as close to East/West as possible. On a sunny day, of course. To heal a scald, dip nine leaves into spring water, lay against the wound saying to each leaf *"The Maiden Bride came out of the East, bearing with Her Fire and Frost. Out Fire, In Frost."* This is obviously the origin of the one I gave you before.

If you wish to have money in your purse, put in it three leaves each of blackberry, bergamot and bistort. It is no wonder, that as it does all these good things, the Blackberry was held in such disapproval by the Church.

Libra

Libra is the Cardinal Air sign which is ruled by Venus and if what has gone before is believed, it is also ruled by Bride. The symbol, the Scales should denote balance and Librans are supposed to be well-balance and of a quiet nature, not liking loud voices or arguments. Something must have gone terribly wrong when I was born, because I can both shout and sing very loudly, I like Wagner played at full blast, although not pop music, and I do enjoy an argument.

The lady who edited the first edition put a load of stuff into it about the Tarot, which I will quote. *"The card is Justice which indicates innate ability* (for what) *and that which guides and urges the Cosmic power represented by the Fool. She carries a sword of steel"*. I was given a beauty for my last birthday.

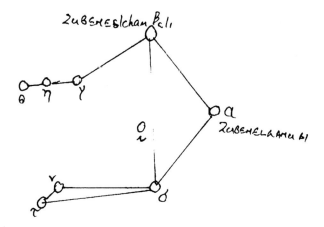

The colour is green and the gem is emerald. Jacquie says that they enhance dreams and meditation. Now I'll drink to this but I'd like influences of prosperity, kindness, tranquillity but also the patience and balance I've never found. Perhaps I should invest in some emeralds.

Michaelmas Bird

The only bird I can find which is related to this time is the Titmouse, better known as the blue tit. Robert Graves, quoting Amergin again, says "*Amergin sang of this month   I am a Hill of Poetry.*" This is the month of the poet, who is the least easily abashed of men just as the blue tit is the least easily abashed of birds. Both band together in companies at this month and go on circuit in search of a liberal hand.

The titmouse climbs spirally up a tree, so the poet also spirals to immortality. The colour for this month is variegated, as we can see in the autumn trees, and variegated is the colour of the blue tit and of the master poet's dress.

Try as I will I cannot find an animal to bring to this month except, perhaps the Cat but I can find no reason for thinking that they should especially be associated with September.

Chapter Ten

Balance

I try to believe in balanced force, which is why I have drawn the Yin-Yang at the head of this chapter. This is a doctrine of perfection and I always come back to the Goddess as the chief deity, because to me the Goddess is simply the Earth, this lovely planet which we treat so badly and which gives us so much. I call Her, quite simply, The Lady and should I need to address Her directly, I say 'Ma'am' very politely. The really lovely thing to me is that I can go to Her directly, wherever I am. There is no need to go to a man-made building, even if it was built, like Chartres, for love, by people giving their time and sometimes their lives, just to be there helping. The great henges and even the early pyramids were built in the same way, from a similar devotion.

The Lady can be sought in a leaf, the scent of a small flower or a raindrop. She can be with you when you watch the moon rise, hear the sea on the shore, listen to a brook and smell the seaweed. It is sometimes difficult to refrain from the Celtic triads, they come so naturally when thinking about the goddess, because the most potent sign is in Her three aspects. Why do we always disregard the fourth? We say, Maiden, Mother and Crone, forgetting the Dark Lady altogether. Or perhaps we don't. Perhaps it is fear of what that fourth is that keeps us dumb about Her.

Yet why should we? We do not ignore the winter merely because it is not always clement, the day is short and there are no leaves about. We do not forget the middle of the night because most of us are asleep. So why ignore the dark of the Moon?

We are told that only evil is worked at this time. With due respect, Cobblers.

We are told to work on Sabbats, at the Full Moon, when all sorts of problems can infect our work. There were more battles fought, more murders committed and more general mayhem thought up at the Full than ever happened in the Dark. Yet folk go out and romp about playing at being witches.

Yes, the Full is beautiful and by all means go out and tell Her so, but leave the magical workings for another day. There is a slack time with the Dark too. The tide has ebbed and there is no power. As in Midwinter the Lady has gone to rest. Just remember that She is also the Goddess of Death and Re-birth.

I begin most of my healing work in the waning moon, because one wants the symptoms to go away. I'm told that this is negative, One should work for improvement. But tell me, what is the use of having an even temperature if the bronchitis is still on the chest? Promotions are fine in their place but "Gettings-rid-of" are just as important.

The God is personified for me. I think of Him, always, as Herne; in the winter as the Hunter, striding across the clear sky with the Yell Hounds, going forth to seek out the lawless; or standing by the great stones with the mist swirling about them; I hear Him in the call of the owl and the cry of the fox and the rutting grunt of the stag. In summer, I think of Him as the Green Lord, the Lord of the forest. Like Pan, the friend and Helper. One sees Him in the Oak, in the buzzard flying with lazy wings on a thermal, in any animal jogging along happily in the sun. But, I do not see Him as a "ramping, raging, raping beast." like Crowley. I always tell people, if they really want to see the horned God, to read the chapter "The Piper at the Gates of Dawn", from the "*Wind in the Willows.*"

Herne is always very special to me and I have had several meetings with Him. There was a waking dream, when I was in a dusty room, the window partly boarded up diagonally. The moon streaming in, and the sound of a horse's hooves in the lane below.

A great branched head looking through the window and a hand taking mine to lead me outside where the horses waited. Where we went, I cannot say.

Another time, going round the corner of a grey stone building. There was deep snow and a dark forest behind; a bright light coming from no visible source and Herne waiting with the horses. On one of these occasions, I looked down at the great hound bounding at my stirrup and the rest of the pack boiling around us. "On, On, my babies" I cried and a laugh to wake the forest went up from the pack and from Herne.

This is something I have found when working with our 'native' aspects of the Godhead. The Middle Eastern ones are all pomp and circumstance and incense and are either bad-tempered or bored if you get something wrong. Ours have a sense of fun, and even of the ridiculous and seem to say:-

"Are you sure you want me there dear? I was over there last time."

They seem to enjoy shuffling about when I get them in the wrong places. *"Rather like musical chairs isn't it? I haven't had so much fun in years."* Then there comes a muffled chuckle and an amused *"Try it again Dear. We have plenty of time."* My temple is nine feet square and having several 12' beings giggling uncontrollably, making chaos worse, but always without malice, is very funny. One has to say *"Come along now. No more nonsense. Life is real, life is earnest. I am ready to begin,"* then there is a *"Hurmmph"* and we get down to business.

A great deal of my work to do with the land is done with the aid of Puck, the Old One and by Oak, Ash and Thorn. Kipling's children in *"Puck of Pook's Hill"* called Puck from the centre of a fairy ring on Midsummer's morning, while holding a spring of oak, ash and thorn; but the Good Old One will come at any time, especially if the work is in aid of his beloved England, for He is one of the Great Ones of Gramarye or Albion and works with the archmage Merlin for the good of the realm. I do believe our own beings work better for us than foreign importations. I do not see the point of uttering names I cannot pronounce with any degree of certainty, either during a rite or at any other time and perhaps, as in Mandarin, the intonation alters the sense, so unless one is a very clever and accomplished linguist, which I am not, one may be asking for quite the wrong thing in quite the wrong tone and one might end up with a cosmic kick up the rumble seat.

So I do not use Greek, Egyptian or even Hebraic god names. I do not even use Norse or Saxon, which I used to be able to read, speak and write. I call the Goddess Lady or Ma'am, and the God Herne or Sir. Puck and Merlin know who they are and while I have no doubt that Merlin could argue semantics on Alpha Centauri and not be misunderstood, I know he understands English.

Ultimately, I think I believe in the Light Beyond the Light. The One Beyond. What my son calls "IT". My "Lady" when expanded beyond Earth becomes one half of the "IT" and the Lord, similarly expanded, the other half.

The negative must always have just a tiny bit of positive and vice versa. Our ultimate creator is not quite the same as the cabbalistic Kether, because we are simple village witches and we do not understand such things and I am the extreme xenophobe and believe sincerely that 'abroad begins at Dover', and I take exception to foreign imports. I have always maintained that these islands have more magic, even if it is a little bit hidden and we have to dig for it, than all the Middle East put together.

There is sense in using Middle Eastern forms if one is a High or Cabbalistic Magician but they are out of place in simple village witchcraft, even naming and calling Elemental Kings is a bit strong. There seems to be little point in calling to Nicxa, Paralda et al, when I have already asked Merlin and Morgan to pay a visit. What would be the point? Where would they all stand, and huge beings, while not recognising time, do appreciate space. I would not wish to offend their dignity for the world by cramping them up together and I do prefer to work with Beings I know.

I use English in all my rites. If I am slightly pie-eyed I might use the odd word of Latin, which I do understand and Anglo-Saxon ditto, but not Enochian. This reminds me of a line in one of Chesterton's poems, when referring to French lords of the Middle Ages *"We like their songs and battles, but we never could say their names."* Perhaps no-one alive can pronounce Enochian and rather like Mandarin, a small mis-pronunciation could be disastrous.

The village witch usually works alone, or with one or two good friends. There are times, naturally, particularly festivals, when we gather as many people as possible and celebrate in much the same way as a more structured group. But, we do the rite on the proper day or the evening before not on the nearest Saturday. Festivals are not times to work, this is done in the small, closed group or alone. It may be done outside under an oak, beside a spring or in a grove in the woods. Robed in a cornfield, in ordinary clothes in the middle of Avebury, or even robed in my own little temple.

My temple has a green carpet, a dark blue ceiling and my son has painted a stone circle round the walls and there isn't a cabbalistic symbol anywhere. Not even a Tree of Life. Not even four Holy Creatures, but dragons, unicorns, wolves and dolphins. Those who have worked there vow it is magical.

The spells come from the work I am doing, especially when the small group is working together. We begin with only an outline of the work to be done and with a firm intention. As we speak round the circle, a phrase might be repeated, picked up by one from another and gradually we find that this embodies the working and repeated, becomes the spell. As this happens we start to walk round the circle repeating the phrase and we find that this works better than writing something out beforehand and trying to commit it to memory.

To a village witch, a Book of Shadows is simply a work book. It should include everything one does but not that done by someone else. Your own thoughts on the work, spells you have made up and used; your meditations and dreams, your pathworkings, your intentions and revelations.

Most witches in the past would have been illiterate, so a book would have been no use at all. They needed only a good memory. Ancient tomes in Latin, Greek or any other language are fine for High Magicians living in attics, but yer average wise woman gathered her herbs from the wayside, because she knew from her own experience which ones to use. She would have had one knife, which she would never have called an 'athame' and whatever pots she possessed. She could not afford special ones and she fitted her spell casting between feeding the pigs, cooking the meals, making potions, laying out the dead and delivering the baby. She would have been the only doctor for miles and she relied upon her own common sense, with an occasional exchange of ideas with the wise women of other villages.

I do the same, although now these wise women are met by letter, phone or at meetings of the local W.I. The knowledge of herbs comes from years of study. The memory is, at times, faulty and requires backing up. I do not lay out the dead and the idea of being present at a birth makes me faint. But the experience is mine, and I have found through experience that witchcraft, to be effective must be simple.

It is quite unnecessary to address "THEM' in long, flowing periods. they know who they are and they have heard it all in every language there is. While I would not dream of whistling them up through my teeth like a taxi I know that they respond just as well to something simple.

They know what you are going to say long before you say it, as soon as the thought comes into your head, let alone committing it to deathless prose and vibrating it soulfully in your throat, and a simple request to rid you of your corns, following a long preamble of that nature is enough to either cause them mild hysterics or aim a thunderbolt for wasting their time. Actually, of course, it is your time you are wasting - time means nothing to them.

Perhaps I should qualify this a bit. I spend a lot of time in the cricket season chanting a spell "Oh God of Cricket. Let's have a wicket." I must also confess that when this does not happen and our opponents build up a massive score, I jump around a lot, swearing a blue streak and yelling "You are not listening, dammit."

This only goes to prove the futility of repeating spells.

Taking a God's name for oneself is fraught with danger. Bob Stewart says, working with one aspect might give you a temporary strength but it will surely have a long term effect on your character, which you might not like after a while and then it might be too late. Far better to use a name from fiction or one you have made up.

At the beginning of this book I mentioned the idea, brought into magic about forty years ago, of nudity. By all means dance around in the nude if you like but I was assured that the old rule was, "Naked shalt thou be in thy rites". This is nonsense. No primitive people goes to meet its God naked. If they only put on flowers, mud, paint or feathers, or even leaves, (see Adam and Eve), they put on something. The idea that nothing can penetrate a layer of clothing is rubbish and the idea that nudity induces equality is patent rubbish. People come in all shapes and sizes, some pleasing to the eye when naked and some, as Christopher Fry said, "*Should be hidden behind judicious rags*". I come firmly into the latter category and so do most of the country witches I know. I couldn't imagine my Granny or any of her cronies appearing unclad for any money and she had been a Gaiety Girl.

Chapter Eleven

FULL CIRCLE
31st OCTOBER

"Gather in, gather in, all that has been herein.
Gather in, gather in so that no trace may be seen.
No trace to mar the tranquil days,
Nor frighten folk not of our ways
Gather in, gather in, All that has been herein."

The Wheel has turned, and we are back at Samhaine. We look back on all we have done and assess it. Was it good or was it bad? We look forward to what we are about to begin, in the coming year. Here at the end we begin the next loop of the spiral. In the course of a year's work we find out a great deal about the world in which we live; the trees, plants and birds of each season but most of all we learn about ourselves for if we do not, nothing else is valid. We grow with each season but if we have not learned then our growing will have been in vain.

We have come back to the end of the year. Once again we play the game of Catch the Leaf, to ensure happy months to come. We prepare our Samhaine fare and our rite and we collect the wood, coal and food which will see us and those for whom we have made ourselves responsible through the winter.

How much will we remember of the fun, laughter and sometimes the tears? We should have written up our notebooks and diaries as we went along so that we can look back to times properly recorded. But most of us will have said "I'll just make quick notes now and fill them in during the winter when the fire is alight, the curtains are drawn against the cold and I can settle down to do all those things I have been putting off throughout the summer."

But, we are not hibernating animals however much we would sometimes like to be. There are still calls upon our time and hospitality and things get left until we can no longer remember just exactly which rite it was when we used outdoor sparklers indoors; or when we were all disturbed during a pathworking by someone scratching his leg. We forget the priestess tripping over the cat, who had sneaked in when no-one was looking and the time when someone swore loudly when he spilled hot wax from a large candle onto his bare foot.

But amusing as these things might be on retrospect, even they should have been noted, because it will remind us to be careful with candles, to put the cat out more firmly; to get the right sparklers and to make sure no-one has an itch in the wrong place or at least, has enough self control not to scratch.

There were many rites in the year which have no great festival. These are the working rites and are for healing and making talismans or potions; because it is the New Moon or even because it has been a nice day. One reason I do not work at a full moon is because it was called a "Bomber's Moon" when I was young and that was not a thing to celebrate.

We have, at the end of our own spiral a death which we have been taught to fear. We have been instructed in the horrors of Hell about the pains and woes of that accursed place. But is it so? Helle, after all was one of the names of Persephone in the Otherworld. She appears on the Gundestrup Cauldron, dropping the souls of the departed into purgatory. But the Cauldron is Kerridwen's and the Cauldron is of Inspiration. Far from dropping them in, She is dipping them - keeping a firm hold on their ankles, to wash away their fears, and all the pain, anguish and anxiety accumulated on this journey on Earth, so that, after their purging - (Middle Latin *Purgatorium* - from Purgare to purge or make pure), they may rest, on beds of asphodel, Greek for daffodil - which in the language of flowers means - regret.

The Celtic heaven, Avalon, as opposed to the Otherworld - Annwn - was a place where apple trees bore both flowers and fruit, as in the quotation on an earlier page. A place where souls could rest without the pains and problems of the past life and go over what had been learned and achieved, so that in due time it could be born into another loop of the spiral, to continue its education.

If one did not learn one's lesson, one would keep coming back like a song, to the same old place. This happens through life. We keep tripping over the same old root until we finally see it is there and do something about it. It may not be pleasant to face, but face it we must, sooner or later, if not in this life then certainly in the next, and by this I mean our next incarnation.

I wrote this verse for a friend whose wife had died and who couldn't face the thought of her being in Hell fire.

> *"Be not afraid, for the Lady bids you come*
> *Here where the trees are full of blossoms and fair fruit.*
> *Where you are washed of pain and being numb*
> *And all the problems of the world are mute.*
>
> *Here you are purged of all your doubts and fears*
> *And the Hag, who is your Mother, dries your tears."*

And finally,

> *"We ask a blessing on the Earth, our home.*
> *All who have been here, are here now*
> *And will be in time to come.*
>
> *We ask the Old gods to bless us when we come*
> *To the end of our own particular dance.*
> *So May It Be.*

The Rite of Chocolate

If you are into serious rituals and High Magic, skip this next section.

Someone sent a rite to me from the USA. It was quite short, but spoke of nougat Hashie and chocolate milk. I thought it a little bland for British tastes so I have expanded it a bit. I spent a couple of days in supermarkets listing names of chocolate bars and boxes of the same, I have used many of them in the rite.

My apologies to the chap who wrote it originally, but I have only ever tasted one Hashie and I was not impressed, besides which I am totally xenophobic. I must also apologise to Cadburys, Frys and all the other makers of our own excellent brands - I haven't taken their names in vain but have used them lovingly and with great respect.

I do hope you have as much fun with this rite as we had.

The Rite of Chocolate

Being the most Ancient and Occult Rite of the Temple of Cosus Cocolaum Unba

The Temple shall be decked with an altar cloth of white linen, covered with brown silk. Silver candlesticks, adorned with cream satin ribbons, in which brown candles will be lit. Upon the pantacle there shall be slices of the cake known as 'Death by Chocolate' and in the chalice there shall be the liquid known as Cadbury's Chocolate Cream.

There shall be incense of Plenty and a pile of Roses in the south.

The athame shall be a great big chocolate eclair. Also on the altar shall be a small dish of mousse and any of the following: Mars Bars, Milky Ways, Walnut Whips, Kit Kats, Bounty and/or Aero.

Lord of the Galaxy now casts the circle using his own words and using the eclair.

Those taking part:

The Lord of the Galaxy
The Lord of Mars
The Lady of the Milky Way
Lady of Delight (otherwise known as Turkish)
Lady Bounty(ful)
The Lady of Darkness

The Rite

Cleanse the sacred space with the bowl of Chocolate sprinkles (those little chocolate bits you use to decorate cakes) or Coco pops (easier to clean up).

Lady of the Milky Way:

> *"Choco-bits where thousands cast*
> *No calories in thy presence last*
> *Let not fat adhere to me*
> *As I will so may it be"*

Lady Bountiful:

> *"Drinking Choc where thou art cast*
> *Turn this milk to chocolate fast*
> *Let all good things now come to me*
> *And make my will all chocolaty"*

Lord of Mars:

> *"Choccie bits, where thou art cast*
> *No calories in Thy presence last*
> *Let no fat adhere to me*
> *And as I will so mote it be"*

210

Lady of the Milky Way:

>*"Aero of the East. Most Holey One*
>*Great Prince of the Palace of Lightness*
>*Be present we pray Thee and guard this circle*
>*From all Moochers approaching from the East"*

Lord of Mars:

>*"Mousse of the South, most creamy One*
>*Great Prince of the Palace of the Dessert*
>*Be present we pray Thee and guard this circle*
>*From all diets approaching from the press"*

Lady Bountiful(ful):

>*"Liquer of the West, Satisfying One*
>*Great Prince of the Palace of Thirst*
>*Be present we pray Thee, and guard this circle*
>*From all Carob approaching from the West"*

Lady of Delight:

>*"Rocky Road of the North, Crunchie One*
>*Great Prince of the Palace of Iced lollies*
>*Be present, we pray Thee, and guard this circle*
>*From all cheap imitations approaching from the North,*
>*South, East of West*

Lady of Darkness:

*"Listen to the words of she who knows the secret of the Black Magic
Box.*

*On the night when you are ravaged by a craving, and better it
should be when your monthly cheque is safely in the bank; then
you shall assemble, three or four together, and bring offerings of
money to the spirit of Me, who is the Queen of all Delight.*

In the marketplace shalt thou assemble, you who crave the solace only I can give. To you, in return for your offerings, I shall show Good Things for your tongue and bring sweetness to your lips. And you shall be freed from depression. Let it be known that these offerings may not be in the guise of Gold Coins, found in a net bag, for these may not be exchanged under pain of my most extreme displeasure. The coin that you must submit must be free from Lindt and of that produced by the Kendal Mint. As a sign that you are truly free, thou shalt anoint thy cheeks and fingers with melted chocolate in the sacred symbols known only to those who travel the path and thou shalt make noises of appreciation and nosh, scoff and feast in My Presence."

Lady Bountiful aka "Coconut cream":

"For Mine is the secret that opens your mouth and Mine is the Ripple that puts a smile on your lips and comfy padding on your hips. I am the gracious Goddess who gives JOY and DELIGHT unto the tummies of women and men. Upon earth I give the knowledge of all things scrumptious and all that is beyond DEATH BY CHOCOLATE. Should this occur when under the influence of the intoxication of Truffles, I can do nothing about it. Sorry, I purpose not your deaths when I purpose your custom.

I do not demand your last ROLO as a sacrifice. I demand only money, for behold, chocolate is big business and all pleasures have to be paid for."

Lady of Delight:

"For Mine is the ECSTASY of the cocoa bean and mine is the JOY of earth, yea, even unto high ORBIT. Be joyful in your REVELS, for mine is the law which you will WISPA as you snack,munch and make yummy noises, and go 'MMM-MMM It MELTS IN YOUR MOUTH AND NOT IN YOUR HAND.' And After Eight, before you leave the sacred market, lick your fingers, do not leave traces to upset those who like not my DELIGHTS, for danger befalls those who drive with sticky fingers. Then go unto your Matchmaker and He will give unto you the Blue Riband of the true

follower. Let none stop you aside for this is a PICNIC that might well turn into a MARATHON."

Lady of the Milky Way:

"Hear now the words of the Goodie Goddess, in the dust of whose feet are the cheap imitations like Hershey Bars. Whose body graces the counters of sweet counters and the finer chocolate shops everywhere, like Thornton's Harrod's and Fortnum's.

I am the beauty of Chocolate Buttons and the satisfying softness of soft centres taken by Moonlight. The mystery of how they get the filling inside chocolate liquers and fill the hearts of all but vegans with desire. Call unto thy Soul Food to arise and come with me. For I am the centre of Nut Whirls. From Me do all confections spring and unto Me thou shalt return again and again and again.

Before My smeared face, beloved of men, women and children, thine innermost being shall be enfolded in the rapture of overdose. Let My taste be within the mouth that rejoices. For behold, all acts of yummieness and pleasure are My rituals. Therefore let there be gooeyness and mess, crispness and the crackling of wrapping paper, big slabs and bite-sized pieces and chocolate covered cherries within you all.

And you who think to seek Me, know that your seeking and yearning shall avail you not, unless you know the mystery "From My darkest Snickers I have fashioned the desire of the Heart" and that which has been with you since you looked up at the sweet counter and said "I like that". I am that which can only be obtained from almost any shop and petrol station in the land. Serve Me by demanding the last Rolo from friend and the unknown passenger upon the bus which taketh you to your destination. Messed be"

Lady of Darkness:

"Hear now the words of the Chocolate God, who has been called Toblerone, Bendicks and the Yorkie Bar Kid."

Lord of the Galaxy:

"I am the strength of Pic and Mix, and when you shalt choose to a Double Take that you may have twice as many. I am the piece-that-fell-on-the-floor-but-may-not-be-too-dusty. I am the bitterness of the Bournville Plain.

No matter how you try to resist, I will hunt you out and I will become your sacred prey. I am the warmth of hot cocoa in winter and the call that leads to the really expensive choc shop in the vortex of the city, but do not Flake out when you have to pay up.

I give you, my greedy ones, the Fire of the Love of Chocolate. The Power of Jaw to bite off the frozen Milky Way. Above all I will give you the comfort of Haargen-das when your love lies unrequited. I instill in you the insight to find that chocolate that was lost and to see a chocolate stand a mile away.

By the power of the half-melted Kit-Kat in the glorious sun, I charge you; by the darkest depths of the bowl of mousse, I charge you; by the furthest chunks of the mighty Yorkie, I charge you and by the perfect swirlyness of the Walnut whip, I charge you, to follow your instinct wheresoever it may lead. For in this path you may come to know the Paths of the Galaxy and the wonders of the Inner Wrapper. For you are mine and I am dear."

Lord of Mars:

"When Twilight falls, take joy in the first bite, the last satisfying slurp. Eat not the baking chocolate or the stuff that is not Dairy Milk.

Leave a little, for by thy gifts shall you please Me and sharing is one of the Quality Streets of Life. though the road be Crunchie ye shall tread it.

I am the Lord of Chocolate and i will never be further away than the 24 hour garage on the corner, (where you might meet a lion, but never a Tiger) or the machine that never works if you are really desperate. I am the spirit of the child who can never get enough. If you are a true Chocolate lover, your spirit and Mine are intertwined."

Follows the blessing of the Cadbury's Cream Liquer

Lord of the Galaxy:

"Be it known that milk chocolate is not better than plain chocolate."

Lady of Darkness:

"Nor is dark chocolate better than milk."

Both together:

"For both are better than Milky Bars and NEITHER ONE IS CAROB."

Lord of the Galaxy:

"As the whipped cream is to the chocolate eclair."

Lady of Darkness:

"So the creamy nougat is to the Milky Way."

Both Together:

"And when they are eaten, they are in truth yummy, for there is no greater delight upon earth than to feast until you are sick, upon chocolate."

Dismiss quarters.

Lady of Darkness:

"We have done this rite in the presence of the Great Goddess."

All: *"**And all because the Lady loves Milk Tray.**"*

FREE DETAILED CATALOGUE

A detailed illustrated catalogue is available on request, SAE or International Postal Coupon appreciated. Titles are available direct from Capall Bann, post free in the UK (cheque or PO with order) or from good bookshops and specialist outlets. Title currently available include:

Animals, Mind Body Spirit & Folklore

Angels and Goddesses - Celtic Christianity & Paganism by Michael Howard
Arthur - The Legend Unveiled by C Johnson & E Lung
Auguries and Omens - The Magical Lore of Birds by Yvonne Aburrow
Book of the Veil The by Peter Paddon
Call of the Horned Piper by Nigel Jackson
Cats' Company by Ann Walker
Celtic Lore & Druidic Ritual by Rhiannon Ryall
Compleat Vampyre - The Vampyre Shaman: Werewolves & Witchery by Nigel Jackson
Crystal Clear - A Guide to Quartz Crystal by Jennifer Dent
Earth Dance - A Year of Pagan Rituals by Jan Brodie
Earth Magic by Margaret McArthur
Enchanted Forest - The Magical Lore of Trees by Yvonne Aburrow
Healing Homes by Jennifer Dent
Herbcraft - Shamanic & Ritual Use of Herbs by Susan Lavender & Anna Franklin
In Search of Herne the Hunter by Eric Fitch
Inner Space Workbook Developing Counselling & Magical Skills Through the Tarot
Kecks, Keddles & Kesh by Michael Bayley
Living Tarot by Ann Walker
Magical Incenses and Perfumes by Jan Brodie
Magical Lore of Animals by Yvonne Aburrow
Magical Lore of Cats by Marion Davies
Magical Lore of Herbs by Marion Davies
Masks of Misrule - The Horned God & His Cult in Europe by Nigel Jackson
Mysteries of the Runes by Michael Howard
Oracle of Geomancy by Nigel Pennick
Patchwork of Magic by Julia Day
Pathworking. A Practical Book of Guided Meditations by Pete Jennings
Pickingill Papers. The Origins of Gardnerian Wicca by Michael Howard
Psychic Animals by Dennis Bardens
Psychic Self Defence - Real Solutions by Jan Brodie
Runic Astrology by Nigel Pennick
Sacred Grove - The Mysteries of the Forest by Yvonne Aburrow
Sacred Geometry by Nigel Pennick
Sacred Lore of Horses The by Marion Davies
Sacred Ring - Pagan Origins British Folk Festivals & Customs by Michael Howard
Secret Places of the Goddess by Philip Heselton
Talking to the Earth by Gordon Maclellan
Taming the Wolf - Full Moon Meditations by Steve Hounsome
The Goddess Year by Nigel Pennick & Helen Field
West Country Wicca by Rhiannon Ryall
Witches of Oz The by Matthew & Julia Phillips

Capall Bann is owned and run by people actively involved in many of the areas in which we publish. Our list is expanding rapidly so do contact us for details on the latest releases.

Capall Bann Publishing, Auton Farm, Milverton, Somerset TA4 1NE.